Cooking with Wine

Betty Dunleavy

Lansdowne

Sydney Auckland London

ACKNOWLEDGEMENTS

Sincere thanks to friends in the food and wine industry for information and assistance; to Pot Pourri Designs, Cremorne Plaza, for generous assistance with photographic accessories; and to my family, my best tasters and most honest critics.

Published by Lansdowne, Sydney
a division of RPLA Pty Limited
176 South Creek Road, Dee Why West, NSW, Australia, 2099

First published by Paul Hamlyn Pty Limited
176 South Creek Road, Dee Why West, Australia 2099
First Published 1979
Reprinted 1985
© Copyright RPLA PTY LIMITED
Produced in Australia by the Publisher
Printed in Hong Kong by
South China Printing Co.

ISBN: 0 7018 1939 1

Contents

GUIDE TO WEIGHTS & MEASURES

The metric weights and metric fluid measures used in this book are those of the **Standards Association of Australia.** A good set of scales, a graduated Australian Standard measuring cup and a set of Australian measuring spoons will be very helpful and can be obtained from leading hardware and kitchenware stores.

All cup and spoon measurements are level:
The **Australian Standard measuring cup** has a capacity of 250 millilitres (250 ml).
The **Australian Standard tablespoon** has a capacity of 20 millilitres (20 ml).
The **Australian Standard teaspoon** has a capacity of 5 millilitres (5 ml).

In all recipes, imperial equivalents of metric measures are shown in parentheses, e.g. 500 g (1 lb) beef. Although the metric yields of cup and weighed measures are approximately 10 per cent greater than the imperial yields, the proportions remain the same. Therefore, for successful cooking use either metric or imperial weights and measures — do not mix the two.

New Zealand, British, United States and Canadian weights and measures are the same as Australian weights and measures except that:
(a) the Australian and British Standard tablespoons have a capacity of 20 millilitres (20 ml) whereas the New Zealand, United States and Canadian Standard tablespoons have a capacity of 15 millilitres (15 ml), therefore all tablespoon measures should be taken generously in those countries;
(b) the imperial pint (Australia, New Zealand and Britain) has a capacity of 20 fl oz whereas the US pint used in the United States and Canada has a capacity of 16 fl oz, therefore pint measures should be increased accordingly in those two countries.
The following charts of conversion equivalents will be useful:

Imperial Weight	Metric Weight
½ oz	15 g
1 oz	30 g
2 oz	60 g
3 oz	90 g
4 oz (¼ lb)	125 g
6 oz	185 g
8 oz (½ lb)	250 g
12 oz (¾ lb)	375 g
16 oz (1 lb)	500 g
24 oz (1½ lb)	750 g
32 oz (2 lb)	1000 g (1 kg)
3 lb	1500 g (1.5 kg)
4 lb	2000 g (2 kg)

Key: oz = ounce; lb = pound; g = gram; kg = kilogram.

Imperial Liquid Measures	Cup Measures	Metric Liquid Measures
1 fl oz		30 ml
2 fl oz	¼ cup	
3 fl oz		100 ml
4 fl oz (¼ pint US)	½ cup	
5 fl oz (¼ pint imp.)		150 ml
6 fl oz	¾ cup	
8 fl oz (½ pint US)	1 cup	250 ml
10 fl oz (½ pint imp.)	1¼ cups	
12 fl oz	1½ cups	
14 fl oz	1¾ cups	
16 fl oz (1 pint US)	2 cups	500 ml
20 fl oz (1 pint imp.)	2½ cups	
32 fl oz	4 cups	1 litre

Key: fl oz = Fluid ounce; ml = millilitre.

OVEN TEMPERATURE GUIDE

The Celsius and Fahrenheit temperatures in the chart below relate to most gas ovens. Increase by 20°C or 50°F for electric ovens or refer to the manufacturer's temperature guide. For temperatures below 160°C (325°F), do not increase the given temperature.

Description of oven	Celsius °C	Fahrenheit °F	Gas Mark
Cool	100	200	¼
Very Slow	120	250	½
Slow	150	300	2
Moderately Slow	160	325	3
Moderate	180	350	4
Moderately Hot	190	375	5
Hot	200	400	6
Very Hot	230	450	8

EQUIVALENT TERMS

Most culinary terms in the English-speaking world can cross national borders without creating havoc in the kitchen. Nevertheless, local usage can produce some problems. The following list contains names of ingredients, equipment and cookery terms that are used in this book, but which may not be familiar to all readers.

Used in this book	Also known as
baking powder	double-acting baking powder
baking tray	baking sheet
beetroot	beets
bicarbonate of soda	baking soda
biscuits	cookies
boiler chicken	stewing chicken
bream	sole
pepper, red or green	sweet or bell pepper, capsicum
caster sugar	fine granulated sugar, superfine sugar
cornflour	cornstarch
desiccated coconut	shredded coconut
essence	extract
eggplant	aubergine
fillet (of meat)	tenderloin
frying pan	skillet
glace (fruits)	candied
grill/griller	broil/broiler
hard-boiled egg	hard-cooked egg
icing sugar	confectioners' sugar
minced (meat, etc.)	ground
mincer	grinder
okra	gumbo, ladies' fingers
pastry	pie crust
pawpaw	papaya
pinch (of salt)	dash
plain flour	all-purpose flour
prawns	shrimps
rosewater essence	rose extract
self-raising flour	self-rising flour
shallots	green onions, scallions
sieve	strain/strainer
(to) sift	(to) strain
snapper	sea bass
spring onions	scallions, green onions
stone, seed, pip	pit
sultanas	seedless raisins
tea towel	dish towel, glass cloth
(to) whisk	(to) whip, beat
zucchini	courgettes

All recipes serve 5–6 unless otherwise stated

Introduction

This book has been written for the homemaker of today who is not only the cook and host or hostess but also the winebuyer. It should provide sufficient information about wine, both in and with the foods selected, to enable you to prepare and serve varied and interesting meals for family or guests.

The 'wine talk' section of the book will help you gain a basic knowledge and understanding of wine. It deals with wine styles, classifications and grape varieties and gives guidance on the selection of wines to serve as an enjoyable accompaniment to a meal.

The recipe sections will give you some knowledge of the variety of ways in which wine can be used as an ingredient in the preparation and cooking of food for all occasions. Not all the recipes are new: some are old favourites, some are certain compliment winners I have used when entertaining, and others are unashamedly 'stolen' from friends — for copy is the greatest form of praise!

Each recipe includes one or more suggestions for the type of wine which would complement the food. It will guide you in the purchase and serving of a wine for that particular dish, at that particular meal. It is not envisaged that a whole menu need be chosen from the recipes in the various sections, only that they will add interest to a meal.

Join me in the wonderful world of good food with wine!

BETTY DUNLEAVY

Wine and Food

It is not necessary to become an expert on food and wine before you can serve good wine and good food together. With just a basic cookery knowledge and a little attention to a few important principles for the use of food and wine, much pleasure can be added to meals, whether they be simple family fare or special guest occasions.

WINE IN FOOD

The secrets of successful cooking with wine are balancing the taste of the wine with the ingredients, the method of using wine in the preparation of the food and the care taken to ensure the completed dish retains its basic tastes, accentuated by the distinctive fragrance and flavour of the wine.

Food and wine flavours should complement each other, neither one dominating nor overpowering the other. Do not be tempted to add a bit more. It is always better to use less, relying on a little extra flavour from the wine to be served with the meal.

Wine becomes a magical ingredient when used in a marinade (soaking liquid), helping to tenderise the fibres of the less expensive cuts of meat, older "chickens" and fuller flavoured game animals and birds. Wine marinades containing herbs, spices and other flavouring agents add an extra richness of flavour to meats for grilling, frying and roasting as well as in soups, stews, pot roasts and casseroles.

Wine can be used as all, or part, of the liquid in recipes requiring boiling, poaching or simmering. In this instance, the main purpose is to first dissipate and evaporate the alcohol in the wine because it will give the food a harsh and unpleasant taste. Once the alcohol has evaporated the wine will impart a distinctive taste to the food, becoming soft and mellow according to the strength of the wine and the cooking time.

Some recipes call for wine to be "cooked" before the other ingredients are added, e.g. cheese fondue. This eliminates the possibility of any unpleasant taste remaining in the dish. Recipes calling for the stronger, more full-bodied wines or shorter cooking times are often improved if the wine is preheated or pre-cooked before being added to the other ingredients.

Sauces are considerably enhanced by the addition of wine. Fruity, robust reds will lift the character and the colour of rich brown sauces for meat, poultry or game. Lighter, refreshing whites in creamy, delicate sauces add a soft piquancy to white meats, fish and vegetables. Relate the taste of wine to the flavour desired for the sauce — a light, crisp, white wine for a light sauce with fish or fowl, a full-flavoured fruity red for a brown beef sauce, a vermouth where a delicate spice or herbal character is needed and a rich sweet wine or concentrated liqueur for sweet desserts.

For logical and economic reasons cook with the same wine that has been chosen for drinking with the meal. There are some practical exceptions to this rule. There may be only sufficient wine to serve your guests. It may be a very special, rare or expensive wine or it may not be practical to open the bottle when you begin cooking, particularly when part preparation may be commenced many hours — or days — ahead of time. In this case use a different wine, but one of a similar taste as the one to be served with the meal.

Leftover wine can be kept, tightly corked, for a few days. Store upright, in the refrigerator or cellar, so that the smallest possible surface area is exposed to the air. A few drops of oil, poured on the surface, will give the wine extra protection from air contact and possible oxidising or souring. This wine would be suitable for cooking only. Acid-tasting, oxidised wines can be used in marinades or salad dressings, provided they have an otherwise agreeable taste.

Never buy cheap wine for cooking — if the wine is not good enough to drink it is not good enough to be used in expensive recipes.

When planning an entire menu, include only one or two dishes cooked in wine.

Flame or Flambé Cookery

Quite distinct from the above uses of wine in cookery is the method of flaming foods — either during the cooking process or as the dramatic finale. It can be the flamboyant touch to earn both envy and acclaim or it can be a best-forgotten failure — depending on the care and attention given to a few important details.

Only liquors with high alcohol content can be used for successful flambe cookery — brandy, gin, whisky, vodka, rum and liqueurs made from brandy, grain spirit and added alcohol.

The alcohol in the liquor, which gives the flames, needs to be released by warming before it flames effectively. If overheated the alcohol will evaporate before the fumes can be ignited. Once ignited, a gentle shaking of the pan will distribute both flames and liquor over the surface of the food.

Flaming foods during the cooking process adds a slight caramelised flavour not obtained by other means. The flaming alcohol will help to burn away excessive fats, dissolve any crust in the bottom of the pan and form a glaze which can become the basis of a special sauce. If the flames leap alarmingly high because of a high fat content in the pan, cover the pan quickly with the lid to suffocate the flames.

Flaming cooked foods at the table as a dramatic finale requires a lot more care — both in the competent handling of the flaming foods with a nearby, wide-eyed audience and the necessity to burn off all the alcohol without over-caramelising the dish before serving. Although it is not necessary to completely cook the added liquor in the pan, any remaining alcohol could leave a harsh, medicinal taste — not often compatible to a sweet dessert.

The head-waiter's trick of sprinkling a little sugar over the food just before flaming produces a better lasting flame and assists to disguise a possible bitter after-taste.

Most liqueurs are concentrated in flavour so that only small amounts are necessary to give the required spicy, fruity or special taste to a particular dish.

A further word of caution. Practice flame cookery well, in the safety of the kitchen and alone — before attempting to perform an impressive presentation in front of guests!

WINES WITH FOOD

The traditional phrase of 'white wines with white meats, red wines with red' is based on the experienced opinions of wine and food lovers throughout the ages. But there are exceptions. Sometimes a white meat may have a piquant, savoury sauce or spicy tasting accompaniment, making the whole dish too strong to balance with a light white wine; or a red meat may be cooked in a creamy sauce with mushrooms or other bland tasting foods, and a red wine may be too dominant in both fragrance and flavour. Some people are confirmed white wine drinkers, and others are red wine enthusiasts. There are those who believe there is only one wine to drink throughout the meal — champagne or sparkling wine.

Choose and drink a wine according to your own particular taste, because that is the one you know you will enjoy. There is such a wonderful variety of white and red table wines that it should be possible to find a wine to please all palates and suit all occasions.

Below each recipe in this book is my suggestion for the type of wine which would complement that dish. This is only meant to be a guide to help you select the wine for the meal — a family get-together or a guest occasion.

When selecting a wine spend a little time inspecting the labels on the bottles. Many winemakers are very helpful to the new and inexperienced wine buyer, stating on the label wine style, grape variety or blend of varieties used, growing areas and particular taste characteristics. This can be of enormous help in assisting the purchaser to make the right choice.

If insufficient information is obtainable from the labels consult the wine merchant or liquor store professional.

Good quality cask or flagon wines have a definite place in the choice of a wine to serve with a meal and should also be considered — particularly when eco-nomy is of paramount importance. For cask wines, pour into carafes or jugs before serving. This looks more elegant and gives the wine a chance to "breathe".

CHEESE AND WINE TASTINGS

The secret of a good cheese and wine tasting is to ensure that the cheese and wines harmonise, that neither one dominates the other. Mild cheeses need mild tasting wines as much as strong, tasty mature cheeses need full bodied, robust wines.

Identify the cheeses and wines so that the tasting may become an informative and enjoyable one. Wines may be identified by bottle label only, but extra details of grape varieties, growing areas and other information will be of interest to the enthusiast.

Arrange cheeses and wines in complementary tasting groups — mild with mild, strong cheeses with robust wine — in separate areas.

Allow about 125 g (4 oz) to 185 g (6 oz) of cheese and three-quarters to 1 bottle of wine per quest. Functions of very large numbers or short periods will require slightly less.

Things to avoid

When selecting your accompaniments there are a number of things to avoid. Don't choose salty biscuits or nuts because these will affect the taste of the cheese and wines. Avoid acid tasting fruits, sugared or crystallised preparations. And lightly rinse any pickled vegetables to remove the acid tasting preserving liquid.

Don't confuse your guests by providing too many cheeses and wines.

7

WINE & CHEESE TASTING CHART

CHEESE GROUPS	RELATED WINES	ACCOMPANIMENTS
Appetizers cream and cottage cheese; feta; mild processed cheeses	sherries, vermouths; rose; cocktails and mixed drinks	prepared dips and spreads; pâté; meats; savouries
Mild Cheeses edam; gouda; swiss; mozzarella; mild cheddars; camembert	moselle; hock, chablis; riesling; rosé	apple, pear wedges; grapes; melon; cucumber and celery sticks
Tasty Cheeses smoked and savoury processed cheeses; provolone; pepato; pecorino; mature and vintage cheddars	riesling; white burgundy; claret or burgundy	green, black olives; shallots or onion; tasty sausage meats; gherkins
Specialty Cheeses blue vein; port wine cheddar; brie; fancy cheeses; potted cheeses	burgundy; port wine muscat; madeira	shallots or onion; celery sticks; radishes; dried fruits; muscatels
Dessert Cheeses cream and cottage cheese; ricotta; sweet fancy cheeses	sauternes; champagne sparkling wines; liqueurs	prepared fruit dips; cheesecake; dates, figs; prunes; nuts

Hors d'Oeuvres and Savouries

FRESH MUSHROOM SAVOURIES

500 g (1 lb) small button mushrooms
250 g (8 oz) cream cheese
1 teaspoon grated horseradish
2 tablespoons dry sherry
salt and pepper
finely chopped parsley or chives
paprika

Remove stems from the mushrooms and wipe over; arrange, cup side uppermost, on a tray. Mix the cream cheese, grated horseradish and sherry well; season to taste with salt and pepper. Fill into the mushroom cups, cover lightly and chill.

Just before serving, sprinkle alternate rows of stuffed mushrooms with chopped parsley or paprika. Arrange on a savoury platter and serve.

Wine suggestions: A medium dry sherry, served slightly chilled, or a dry vermouth over ice cubes would complement the tang of the horseradish in the mushroom filling.

HOT SALMON STRIPS

250 g (8 oz) cream cheese
¼ cup dry vermouth
1 x 220 g (7 oz) can red salmon
¼ cup finely chopped shallots or spring onions
¼ teaspoon grated horseradish
½ cup sour cream
toasted bread strips, buttered
paprika

Combine the cream cheese with the vermouth, blending through; add the drained boneless salmon, shallots and horseradish. Stir the sour cream through, spread into a small greased ovenproof dish and bake in a moderate oven for 20-25 minutes.

Spread hot mixture onto buttered toast strips, sprinkle with paprika and arrange on a serving platter. Serve hot.

Wine suggestions: For a short aperitif choose a delicate flor fino sherry; for a longer drink a chilled hock style wine with its fresh clean aftertaste would balance the distinctive salmon taste.

HAM 'N' CHEESE SLICES

2 cups grated Cheddar cheese
125 g (4 oz) packaged cream cheese
2 tablespoons chopped chives
¼ cup dry vermouth
2 cups very finely diced ham sausage
savoury biscuits, buttered

Combine the grated cheese, cream cheese and chives in a bowl and mash with a fork to blend well. Gradually work in the vermouth and chill for 30-40 minutes to firm. Form into a long roll about 4 cm (1½ inches) in diameter.

Spread the diced ham on a sheet of aluminium foil, place the cheese roll on top and roll firmly to coat all sides: press sausage pieces in firmly. Roll in the foil, wrap and chill for 2-3 hours.

Just before serving, remove foil, cut the roll into slices and arrange on the buttered biscuits.

Wine suggestions: A dry vermouth served over ice or a bianco vermouth served with soda and lemon garnish would suit the mild savoury flavour.

CRABMEAT BOUCHÉES

1 x 200 g (7 oz) can crabmeat
¾ cup thick sour cream
¼ cup egg mayonnaise
½ cup finely chopped shallots or spring onions
1 cup chopped seeded cucumber
1 cup finely shredded watercress or lettuce
2 tablespoons dry vermouth
salt
tabasco sauce
30 small short pastry or bread cases
paprika

Drain the crabmeat, removing any bony pieces; flake and combine with the next five ingredients. Add the vermouth, mix well; add salt and tabasco to season well; cover and chill.

Just before serving, warm the pastry or bread cases – do not overheat – and spoon the chilled crabmeat in equal portions into each case. Sprinkle lightly with paprika, arrange on serving platter and serve.

Wine suggestions: A delicate tasting dry vermouth would compliment the seafood taste, both in and with these savouries. Or serve a chilled, chablis style wine with a clean dry finish.

CHEESE TOASTIES

8-9 thick slices sandwich bread
1 cup white wine
3 eggs
1 cup grated Parmesan cheese
1 teaspoon dry mustard
½ cup melted butter
cayenne pepper

Lightly trim the crusts from the bread and cut each slice into 3-4 finger lengths. Pour the wine into a shallow dish and dip the bread fingers quickly into the wine so they absorb a little.

Beat the eggs, add the grated cheese and mustard and mix thoroughly; brush generously all over each bread finger, coating them well.

Arrange the bread finger on a well-greased scone tray, drizzle the melted butter over each and sprinkle sparingly with cayenne.

Bake in a moderately hot oven for 10-12 minutes, turn the fingers and bake a further 5-7 minutes until golden brown and crisp. Serve hot.

Wine suggestions: This 'cheese on toast' savoury with its tangy taste would suit a full flavoured riesling or white burgundy, served chilled.

APPLE CHEESE WEDGES

125 g (4 oz) blue vein cheese
60 g (2 oz) butter, softened
2 tablespoons brandy
4 firm red apples
1 tablespoon water
1 tablespoon lemon juice

Combine the cheese, butter and brandy and blend well; cover and chill overnight to soften the flavours.

Cut the unpeeled apples into wedges, removing the core; quickly dip into lemon water to prevent discolouration. Drain and dry apples, spread one side with the cheese mixture and arrange on a platter; serve cold.

Wine suggestions: The strong, biting taste of the blue vein cheese needs an aperitif with a clean dry finish: a slightly chilled flor sherry or an aromatic dry vermouth, served over ice.

Savoury platter (clockwise): Mushrooms a la russe, recipe on page 14; Prosciutto fritters, recipe on page 13; Ginger Pork Appetizers, recipe on page 13; Cheese Almond Balls, recipe on page 12; Ham 'n' Cheese Slices, recipe on page 9.

CHEESE ALMOND BALLS

2 rounds Camembert or Brie cheese
1 cup white wine
250 g (8 oz) butter, softened
1½ cups grated Swiss cheese
1½ cups finely chopped almonds
salt and cayenne pepper
1 tablespoon butter, melted

Remove the rind from the cheese and place in a shallow dish; pour the wine over and marinate overnight, turning the cheese occasionally to absorb the wine.

Force the cheese through a fine sieve into a bowl, add the softened butter and grated cheese and blend well; chill 2-3 hours. Form teaspoons of the mixture into balls with cool, wetted hands; chill again. Place the chopped almonds in a scone tray, sprinkle salt and cayenne sparingly over and drizzle with melted butter.

Toast under heated griller, shaking the pan frequently, until light golden brown; remove and cool.

Roll the cheese balls in the almonds to coat all over, then store in the refrigerator until ready to serve.

Wine suggestions: The mild, slightly sweet combination of the cheese and almonds in these little savouries would be complemented by a chilled white wine of the fruity moselle style.

PIZZA ROLLETTES

1 x 250 g (8 oz) packet pizza mix
2 teaspoons dried oregano
½ cup finely diced salami
½ cup finely diced smoked ham
1 cup finely diced mortadella sausage
½ cup shredded mozzarella cheese
½ cup cream or cottage cheese
2 tablespoons dry vermouth
egg or 1 tablespoon milk for glazing
grated Parmesan cheese
2 tablespoons dry vermouth (extra)

Make up the pizza dough according to directions on the packet to the stage of standing aside to rise; allow the dough to double in size. Turn onto a floured board and roll out to a large thin rectangle approx. 30 cm (12 in) x 23 cm (9 in). Cut into three equal strips 10 cm (4 in) wide.

Scatter the oregano evenly across the surface of the dough. Combine the finely diced meats with the shredded mozzarella and softened cream cheese; add the wine and mix well.

Spread the meat mixture in a thin line down the centre of each dough strip and brush down one side with egg or milk glazing; roll up with the join on the underside.

Cut each roll into small rollettes and place on a greased scone tray; brush each rollette with egg glazing and bake in a hot oven for 12-15 minutes. Remove. Combine the canned pizza filling mixture with the grated cheese and extra vermouth in a saucepan, heat until boiling. Serve the rollettes with the sauce for dipping.

Wine suggestions: The stronger savoury flavourings in the filling of these little rolls call for an accompanying drink of equal taste – a full amontillado sherry or a chilled dry rosé.

PROSCIUTTO FRITTERS

125 g (4 oz) prosciutto ham, thinly sliced
¾ cup white wine
¼ cup dry vermouth
60 g (2 oz) butter or substitute
¼ teaspoon salt
pinch cayenne pepper
1 cup plain flour, sifted
3 large eggs, beaten
½ cup grated Cheddar cheese
¼ cup grated Parmesan cheese
oil for frying

Chop the ham into small dice. Combine the wines, butter and salt in a saucepan; bring to the boil, sprinkling the cayenne over. Add the flour all at once and beat vigorously to combine all ingredients. Reduce the heat and continue stirring until the mixture leaves the sides of the saucepan; remove and set aside for 2 minutes.

Gradually add quantities of the well beaten eggs, beating until all the egg is absorbed before adding a further quantity. Add the ham and grated cheeses and beat through.

Drop heaped teaspoons of the batter into heated oil and fry until well browned on both sides. Drain on absorbent paper and serve hot.

Wine suggestions: A well chilled wine – a rosé with a dry clean finish or a riesling – would act as both a temperature contrast and a thirst quencher with these hot fried savouries.

GINGER PORK APPETIZERS

1 kg (2 lb) finely minced pork
1 cup soft white breadcrumbs
1 egg, beaten
salt and pepper
½ cup soy sauce
1 cup water
½ cup finely diced onion
2 tablespoons brown sugar
¼ cup sweet sherry
1 clove garlic, crushed
2 teaspoons grated ginger root
few drops hot chilli sauce
1 tablespoon cornflour
2 tablespoons water (extra)
½ cup peanut oil

Combine the minced pork, breadcrumbs and beaten egg with salt and pepper; mix well and form into small balls with wetted hands.

Place on a greased baking dish and part-cook in a moderate oven for 30 minutes; lift out and transfer to shallow china or glass dish.

Combine the soy sauce with the following 7 ingredients in a saucepan; heat until boiling. Reduce heat and simmer 10-12 minutes. Blend the cornflour with extra water, stir into the soy sauce mixture to thicken. Add the peanut oil, mix through and allow to cool.

Pour over the pork balls, cover and marinate for 2-3 hours, turning from time to time.

Lift pork balls out of marinade, place on aluminium foil on griller tray and cook under heated griller for 7-10 minutes, turning and brushing with the marinade. Transfer to serving platter and serve hot with wooden picks for spearing.

Wine suggestions: The sweet yet spicy flavour of the marinade calls for a medium sweet sherry or a full-bodied white burgundy.

CAMEMBERT EN CROÛTE

2 small Camembert cheeses
2 cups white wine
1 x 375 g (12 oz) packet puff pastry
1 egg yolk
1 tablespoon water
coarse salt

Lightly scrape the surface of each cheese and prick over with a needle or fine skewer. Set each cheese in a small bowl, pour 1 cup wine over, cover and set aside for 1-2 hours; turning from time to time.

Divide pastry in halves and roll each out on a floured board to a square approx. 17 cm (7 in); trim the edges.

Remove the cheeses from the wine; drain and pat dry, then place one in the centre of each pastry square. Lift the points of the pastry square up and over the cheese; combine egg yolk and water and seal the joins with this glazing.

Carefully place the pastries join side down on a greased scone tray; brush egg glazing over the surface. Slash 2-3 air vents in the top of the pastry, scatter coarse salt over and bake in a hot oven for 17-20 minutes, until the pastry is golden brown and cooked through.

Remove to a wire rack and allow to cool for 20-25 minutes to re-firm the cheese; do not chill. Place on serving platter and cut into wedges to serve.

Wine suggestions: A moselle style white wine, used both for the recipe and for the accompanying drink, provides a soft mild taste which would not dominate the delicate flavour of the cheese.

MUSHROOMS À LA RUSSE

2 cartons sour cream
2 tablespoons brandy
2 tablespoons chopped chives
30-36 small button mushrooms
4 hard-cooked eggs, shelled and sliced
40 g (1½ oz) black caviar

Turn the sour cream into a muslin-lined strainer and drain well overnight. Combine with the brandy and chives and set aside for 30 minutes.

Remove stems from the mushrooms, wipe the cups over and arrange, cup uppermost on a platter; top with egg slices.

Spoon sour cream mixture onto each of the mushrooms; top with a sprinkling of caviar. Chill until ready to serve.

Wine suggestions: These simple savouries with the elegant touch of caviar would be ideal to serve with a well chilled, dry to medium dry champagne or sparkling wine.

Entrées, Soups and Snacks

HAM CROQUETTES WITH RAISIN SAUCE

3 cups hot mashed potato
60 g (2 oz) butter or substitute, softened
2 egg yolks
1½ cups finely diced cooked ham
2 hard-cooked eggs, shelled and chopped
flour
½ cup evaporated milk
1½ cups dry white breadcrumbs
oil for frying

RAISIN SAUCE

1 cup raisins
1 cup sweet sherry
½ cup water
¼ cup brown sugar
1 teaspoon prepared mustard
2 tablespoons chutney
1 tablespoon wine vinegar
3 teaspoons cornflour, blended in little water

Combine mashed potato with butter and egg yolks, beat until smooth, then fold in diced ham and eggs. Form into 10-12 croquettes, using a little flour. Brush well with evaporated milk, coat with breadcrumbs and place on a platter; chill at least 30 minutes to firm.

Heat oil in a deep saucepan, deep fry croquettes a few at a time until golden brown and crisp; drain well and keep hot.

Combine the raisins and sweet sherry, heat slowly to plump the raisins. Add the following 5 ingredients, bring to the boil and simmer 10 minutes. Thicken with blended cornflour and simmer a further 2-3 minutes. Serve with the ham croquettes.

Note: The ham mixture could also be formed into small balls, deep fried and served as a savoury with the sauce for dipping.

Wine suggestion: The sweet yet spicy sauce accompanying these ham croquettes would go well with a bottled moselle, a flagon moselle or a bottled rosé, depending on when they are to be served.

PORK KIDNEYS IN CREAM SAUCE

4-5 pork kidneys
salted water
flour
salt and pepper
dry mustard
60 g (2 oz) lard or butter
3-4 thick rashers bacon, rind removed
1 teaspoon chopped fresh thyme
½ cup dry sherry
½ cup white wine
½ cup sour cream
½ cup egg mayonnaise
rice cooked in chicken stock for serving
chopped parsley for garnish

Skin and halve kidneys, remove the centre cores and place in salted water. Bring to the boil, drain and repeat in fresh salted water; drain, cool and cut into thick slices.

Toss the kidney slices in flour, well seasoned with salt, pepper and mustard. Sauté kidneys in heated lard with pieces of bacon of similar size for 2 minutes, turning frequently. Add the thyme, sherry and wine; bring to the boil, then simmer, covered for 8-10 minutes.

Swirl the cream and mayonnaise into the pan, heat until just boiling. Adjust seasonings as required and spoon piping hot on individual portions of rice, cooked in chicken stock until just tender. Garnish with chopped parsley and serve immediately.

Note: Subsitute veal kidneys, omitting the blanching process, if preferred.

Wine suggestions: The very rich flavour of the pork kidneys in this entrée require a wine with some strength of character, perhaps a varietal wine made from Traminer or Blanquette grapes.

FAVOURITE CHICKEN PÂTÉ

125 g (4 oz) butter
500 g (1 lb) chicken livers, trimmed
125 g (4 oz) open flat mushrooms
1 tablespoon chopped fresh parsley
1 teaspoon chopped fresh thyme
1 teaspoon salt
½ teaspoon pepper
½ cup red wine
2 tablespoons brandy
125 g (4 oz) butter, melted and cooled
slices of thin toast for serving

Heat 125 g (4 oz) butter in a large frying pan, add the coarsely chopped chicken livers with the sliced mushrooms and sauté, turning frequently, for 1 minute. Scatter the parsley and thyme over the top, with the salt and pepper, pour the wine over and mix through. Cover the pan and simmer for a few minutes – do not overcook the chicken livers.

Heat the brandy in a small pan, ignite and carefully pour over the chicken mixture; shake the pan to distribute the brandy. When the flame dies, cover the pan and set aside to cool.

Spoon quantities of the mixture into a blender and purée, adding a portion of the melted cooled butter to each quantity.

Spoon mixture into a straight sided dish, cover tightly and chill for 1-2 days before use.

Carefully turn out onto a flat platter, garnish as desired. Cut into slices for serving with thin slices of toasted bread.

Wine suggestions: A dry vermouth over ice would provide a delicate, slightly aromatic taste to team with the subtle flavour of the pâté. Or, if desired, a chablis wine.

KIDNEY AND BACON SOUP

375 g (12 oz) beef kidneys
salted water
2-3 thick rashers bacon, rind removed
30 g (1 oz) bacon dripping
1½ cups red wine
1½ cups beef stock
2 bay leaves
1 sprig parsley
1 onion, skinned and chopped
1 teaspoon salt
¼ teaspoon pepper
1 x 440 g (14 oz) can cream of mushroom soup
sour cream for serving
chopped parsley for garnish

Cut the kidneys in halves and soak in salted water for 30 minutes; drain and chop roughly. Cut the bacon into rough pieces and fry in the heated dripping until the bacon fat is transparent.

Add the kidneys and fry, turning constantly, for 1-2 minutes; stir in the wine and bring to the boil. Add the stock with the following 5 ingredients, cover and simmer for 50-60 minutes.

Discard the bay leaves and parsley and lift out a few pieces of kidney and bacon for garnishing.

Press the mixture through a fine sieve, return to the saucepan and stir in the mushroom soup. Simmer 15-20 minutes, spoon into heated bowls and garnish with sour cream, kidney, bacon and chopped parsley. Serve hot.

Wine suggestion: Use a full fruity red wine in the making of the soup; depending on the wines to be served with the main meat course, you may prefer not to serve wine with the soup. If serving as a supper dish with hot crusty bread, a good dry red wine would be suitable.

Favourite Chicken Pâté, recipe on page 16.

CHESTNUT PUFFS

2 stalks celery, finely chopped
2 white onions, skinned and finely chopped
60 g (2 oz) butter or substitute
2 tablespoons flour
1 x 440 g (14 oz) can unsweetened chestnut
  purée
½ cup madeira wine
5 eggs, separated
salt and pepper
butter
breadcrumbs
paprika

Sauté the chopped celery and onions in the heated butter until softened but not browned; stir the flour through and simmer 1 minute. Remove from heat, add the chestnut purée, wine and egg yolks and beat well. Season as required with salt and pepper.

Beat the egg whites until firm but not stiff, lightly fold into the chestnut mixture.

Generously butter the insides of small individual soufflé dishes, sprinkle with breadcrumbs.

Spoon equal portions of the chestnut mixture into each dish, sprinkle paprika over the top and bake in a moderate oven for 25-30 minutes – until just firm. Serve immediately.

Wine suggestions: A soft moselle style wine with good fruit flavour would make an interesting accompaniment to this unusual entrée; or serve a chilled Frontignan wine.

FETTUCINI SICILIENNE

500 g (1 lb) fettucini noodles
salted water
60 g (2 oz) butter or substitute
2 tablespoons olive oil
4 small onions
2 cloves garlic
1 green capsicum
1 x 45 g (1½ oz) can anchovies
1 x 500 g (1 lb) can tomatoes
2 teaspoons chopped fresh basil or marjoram
1 cup white wine
500 g (1 lb) cod or mullet fillets
salt and pepper

Cook the noodles in plenty of salted water until just tender; drain and set aside to keep hot. Heat butter and oil in a large saucepan, add the skinned and chopped onions, crushed garlic and seeded, chopped capsicum and fry until the vegetables are softened. Stir in the chopped anchovies (with oil), tomatoes (with juices), basil and wine. Add the fish, skinned and cut into thin strips, and bring to the boil; season. Cover and simmer for 10-15 minutes.

Toss the noodles with half of the fish sauce and spoon into deep heated bowls. Spoon the remaining sauce over each portion and serve hot as a substantial entrée or hearty snack.

Wine suggestion: This seafood flavoured savoury snack would be ideal accompanied by a light red wine, preferably made from Shiraz or Hermitage grapes.

CHEESE RABBIT ROYALE

2 x 185 g (6 oz) cans tuna in brine
125 g (4 oz) butter or substitute
3 tablespoons flour
1¼ cups evaporated milk
⅓ cup dry sherry
1 cup grated Cheddar cheese
salt and cayenne pepper
4 hard-cooked eggs, shelled and quartered
5-6 crumpets or muffins
extra butter
parsley for garnish

Open the tuna cans, drain and keep separate. Heat the butter in a saucepan, add the flour and blend through; slowly stir in the evaporated milk away from heat. Return to low heat and cook, stirring constantly, until thickened and bubbling. Add the sherry and gradually fold in the grated cheese, cooking only until the cheese has melted; season well. Fold in one can of tuna, heat through, then fold in the quartered eggs, being careful not to break them too much.

Toast the crumpets, butter and spoon equal portions of the remaining tuna on each; reheat slightly. Spoon cheese sauce over each crumpet on warmed plates; garnish with parsley and serve.

Wine suggestion: This quick and easy snack would be well accompanied with a glass of chilled white wine from a good flagon or cask – moselle or riesling style.

CAULIFLOWER CRÈME

4 cups rich chicken stock, strained
1 cup white wine
1 x 500 g (1 lb) cauliflower
2-3 leeks, white sections
2 large potatoes, peeled
1¼ cups cream
salt and white pepper
nutmeg
90 g (3 oz) butter
chopped chives for garnish

Pour the chicken stock and wine into a large saucepan, add the thinly sliced cauliflower, leeks and potatoes and bring to the boil. Cover, reduce heat and simmer for 20-25 minutes, until the vegetables are soft enough to mash easily.

Allow to cool sufficiently to handle easily. Press mixture through a very fine sieve or spoon quantities into a blender to purée; chill until ready for use. Return to the saucepan and reheat over low heat until just commencing to boil.

Stir in the cream and taste, adding salt, pepper and nutmeg as required. Spoon into heated bowls and place a dot of butter on each; swirl around and sprinkle with chives (or extra nutmeg). Serve hot.

Wine suggestion: For a short accompanying drink for this soup choose a medium dry sherry; for a longer one, a chilled chablis, light and dry with an agreeable acid finish.

MUSHROOM SOUP ITALIENNE

60 g (2 oz) butter or substitute
2 tablespoons olive oil
2 small onions, skinned
1 clove garlic, bruised
500 g (1 lb) mushrooms
2 tablespoons tomato paste
2 tablespoons sweet vermouth
3 cups well seasoned chicken stock
2 tablespoons chopped fresh basil
4 egg yolks
½ cup grated Parmesan cheese
5-6 thick slices Italian bread

Heat butter and olive oil in a large pan until foaming; add finely sliced onion and garlic and cook over moderate heat until the onions are nicely browned. Discard the garlic and add the thinly sliced mushrooms; cook, turning constantly, until the mushrooms are softened. Add the tomato paste, vermouth and chicken stock, stir well and bring to the boil; simmer 10-12 minutes.

Beat the chopped basil and egg yolks together, add the grated cheese. Toast the bread slices on one side only and place one in each heated soup bowl; keep hot.

Beat the egg mixture into the soup in a steady stream; when boiling, spoon over the bread slices and serve hot.

Wine suggestion: The slight overall sweetness of this interesting soup would be complemented by the nutty character of a flor sherry.

CHILLED TOMATO SOUP

1 x 470 g (15 oz) can peeled tomatoes
2 young carrots, shredded
1 white onion, skinned and finely chopped
1 bay leaf, broken
1 sprig basil, bruised
2-3 strips lemon peel
6 peppercorns
3 cups clear chicken stock
1 teaspoon sugar
½ cup dry vermouth
salt and pepper
1 orange
sour cream for serving

Place tomatoes with juice, carrots, onion, bay leaf, basil, lemon peel and peppercorns in a large saucepan; bring to the boil, then simmer 8-10 minutes. Strain through fine mesh, return liquid to the saucepan and add stock, sugar and vermouth. Heat until boiling, simmer 5 minutes and add salt and pepper to taste.

Peel 2-3 thin strips of rind from the orange, cut rind into very fine shreds and set aside for garnish. Add strained juice of the orange to saucepan, cool and chill. Serve in chilled bowls with a dollop of sour cream and a sprinkling of orange shreds on each portion.

Wine suggestion: A medium dry sherry – perhaps an amontillado – would provide plenty of flavour to team with this warm weather meal starter.

SWISS CHEESE ON TOAST

5-6 very thick slices white bread
¾ cup white wine
1½ cups shredded Gruyère cheese
1 large egg
¼ teaspoon paprika
¼ teaspoon pepper
3-4 onions, skinned
60 g (2 oz) butter
salt and pepper

Moisten the slices of bread with half the wine and arrange on a well-greased scone tray.

Combine the remaining wine with the cheese, beaten egg and seasonings; spread in equal portions on the bread. Bake in a hot oven until the cheese begins to melt.

Meanwhile sauté the thinly sliced onions in the heated butter until softened and lightly browned; add salt and pepper. Serve the cheese toast hot with a few onion slices arranged on each.

Wine suggestion: A light white wine, perhaps a young riesling, or a chilled dry finish rosé, would be an ideal accompaniment to this filling snack.

BAKED MUSHROOM MOUNDS

10-12 large mushroom cups
5-6 teaspoons brandy
60 g (2 oz) butter or substitute
¼ cup diced shallots or spring onions
¼ cup tomato purée
½ cup finely chopped cooked chicken
2 hard-boiled eggs, shelled and chopped
2 tablespoons dry sherry
salt and pepper
2 teaspoons chopped fresh basil or oregano
2 tablespoons sour cream
dried white breadcrumbs

Remove the stems from the mushrooms, wipe the cups over and sprinkle ½ teaspoon brandy into each, set aside 10 minutes.

Heat the butter until foaming, add the shallots and sauté until softened. Stir in the tomato purée, chicken, eggs and sherry; season with salt and pepper to taste.

Add the basil and sour cream and pile mixture into each mushroom cup; sprinkle with breadcrumbs.

Place in a greased baking dish and cook in a moderate oven for 15-20 minutes. Serve hot.

Wine suggestions: A white wine made from the Pinot Chardonnay grape would have sufficient body and flavour for the variety of savoury tastes in these mushrooms.

Veal Steak and Kidney Flambé, recipe on page 22.

Flambés and Fondues

CHAMPAGNE CHEESE FONDUE

125 g (4 oz) butter
500 g (1 lb) grated mild Cheddar cheese
1½ cups champagne
salt and pepper
truffles, thinly sliced
spears of toasted bread
melted butter

Heat butter in a fondue pot over a low heat and add cheese; stir until melted. Gradually stir in the champagne, add salt and pepper to taste. Stir the thinly sliced truffles through. Brush spears of bread with melted butter and dry them in the oven. Guests dip these into the cheese, twist to coat the tip with fondue.

Wine suggestions: A dry or demi-sec champagne would harmonize with the flavour of the cheese in this fondue; or use a dry sparkling wine. Serve with the same wine.

OYSTER-CHEESE FONDUE

60 g (2 oz) butter or substitute
1 cup white wine
1 x 440 g (14 oz) can cream of oyster soup
250 g (8 oz) shredded Swiss cheese
½ teaspoon dry mustard
1 tablespoon cornflour
salt and cayenne pepper
24-30 shelled oysters
French bread

Heat butter in a fondue pot, add wine and oyster soup and stir over low heat until blended and bubbling. Combine cheese, mustard and cornflour, sprinkle with salt and cayenne. Gradually add quantities of the cheese mixture to the soup and wine, stirring until each quantity has melted and blended through. Add the drained oysters and allow to heat through. Serve with crusty bread chunks for dipping.

Wine suggestions: A white wine of the hock or riesling style would offset the slight sweet taste of the Swiss cheese and oysters in this fondue. Serve with a similar wine.

VEAL STEAK AND KIDNEY FLAMBÉ

500 g (1 lb) veal steak
3 veal kidneys
90 g (3 oz) butter or substitute
4-5 shallots or spring onions
125 g (4 oz) button mushrooms
2 teaspoons chopped fresh rosemary
½ cup brandy
½ cup dry sherry
salt, pepper and mustard
1½ cups sour cream
buttered toast triangles

Slice veal steak across the grain in wafer-thin slices; remove cores from kidneys, rinse and slice thinly. Heat butter in a shallow pan, add veal steak and kidneys and sauté, turning constantly, for 2-3 minutes. Remove with slotted spoon and set aside. Add the sliced shallots and mushrooms to the pan and fry; turning frequently, until softened; add the rosemary. Return the meats to the pan and cook over high heat for 1 minute. Pour combined brandy and dry sherry into the pan, warm and ignite. Allow the flames to die down and add salt, pepper and mustard to taste. Swirl the sour cream through and heat without boiling. Serve at once with triangles of toast.

Wine suggestion: The dry sherry adds an extra touch to the flavour of the brandy in the flambé part of this entrée. Serve with a fresh hock style wine.

CLASSIC CHEESE FONDUE

For each person:
½ clove garlic
⅓ cup white wine
1½ cups lightly packed shredded cheese,
   mixed Gruyère and Emmenthal
1 teaspoon potato flour or cornflour
⅛ cup Kirsch
pepper and nutmeg
approx. 2 cups crusty white bread cubes

Rub the inside of a porcelain or enamel-lined casserole with garlic; add white wine and heat slowly until hot but not boiling; simmer a few minutes. Gradually add portions of cheese, stirring constantly until each portion blends into the wine. Blend the potato flour with the Kirsch, add to the cheese mixture and continue stirring over low heat until the fondue commences to bubble. Add pepper and nutmeg to taste and transfer the casserole dish to a fondue burner or table warmer for serving.

Provide long fondue forks for guests to impale the bread cubes, and swirl in the cheese fondue.
Note: Add extra warmed wine if the fondue becomes too thick. Australian Swiss cheese may substitute for the imported cheeses as desired.

Wine suggestions: A young dry white wine with some acid content, of the chablis or riesling style, will assist with the digestion of the quantity of cheese consumed. Finish with a Kirsch.

BACCHUS BEEF FONDUE

1 kg (2 lb) yearling round or topside steak in
   one piece
3 cups water
1 cup red wine
1 packet onion soup mix
1 bayleaf, broken
few sprigs thyme, basil or marjoram
few peppercorns, crushed
¾ cup olive oil
1 cup sour cream, chilled
2-3 teaspoons grated horseradish
2-3 tablespoons milk
2 tablespoons chopped chives
thick bread crusts

Cut steak into 2.5 cm (1 in) cubes, trimming off all fat and gristle. Pour water and wine into a fondue pot, add onion soup mix and heat through, stirring constantly. Add seasonings, lower heat and simmer 10 minutes; stir the oil through. Combine sour cream with horseradish and milk to give a piquant taste and whipped cream consistency; add chives and chill well.

Guests spear steak cubes onto fondue forks, dip them into the bubbling liquid stock and cook until done to individual taste; then drain lightly, transfer to plate, dip in sour cream mixture and eat.
Note: Crusts of bread dropped into the stock help to eliminate sputtering. Additional dipping sauces; serve well chilled:
Mayonnaise, seasoned with prepared mustard and chilli sauce.
Hollandaise sauce, seasoned with chutney and wine vinegar or lemon juice.
Cream cheese, softened with milk and seasoned with diced cucumber and ground cummin.
White sauce, seasoned with devilled ham spread and anchovy sauce.
Peanut butter, seasoned with soy sauce, chilli sauce and sesame seeds.

Wine suggestions: A full bodied dry red wine with strong fruit flavour would provide sufficient 'lift' to the boiling stock for the beef cube cookery; serve a burgundy style wine.

Seafoods

GRILLED WHOLE FISH WITH WINE BUTTER SAUCE

5-6 whole flounder or similar fish
1 lemon
1½ cups white wine
salt and pepper
melted butter
4-5 spring onions or shallots
125 g (4 oz) butter
1 tablespoon lemon juice

Cut the fins from the fish and remove any scales; rinse the cavity well. Make an incision in the skin just above the tail with the point of a sharp knife; insert a finger in under the skin and loosen all around the edges of the fish. Pull whole skin away from fish, using salt on the fingers for a firmer grip. Place the fish in a shallow dish with a few slices of lemon; pour wine over and allow to marinate for 30-40 minutes, turning frequently. Remove fish, pat dry and sprinkle with salt and pepper on both sides; brush liberally with melted butter. Place the fish on a rack under a heated griller and cook under moderate heat for 7-10 minutes, brushing frequently with melted butter and turning once or twice as required; keep hot.

Pour the wine marinade into a saucepan and bring to the boil; boil for 1 minute and remove the lemon slices.

Add the sliced onions to the wine and boil for a further 1-2 minutes. Remove from the heat and gradually stir in the butter, cut into small pieces. Add the lemon juice and freshly ground pepper to taste. Serve the fish with creamed potatoes and buttered greens, spooning a little sauce over each.

Wine suggestion: This simple classic seafood entrée or main course dish would be complemented by a white varietal wine of full distinctive flavour, a Chenin Blanc or a Sauvignon Blanc.

SHERRIED CRABMEAT ENTRÉE

1½ cups cooked or frozen spinach
2 cups grated mild Cheddar cheese
2 cups cooked flaked crabmeat
5-6 spring onions or shallots
1 cup sour cream
½ cup egg mayonnaise
¼ cup dry sherry
salt and pepper
pinch nutmeg
½ cup soft breadcrumbs
60 g (2oz) butter or substitute
parsley and lemon garnish

Drain the spinach well and arrange in 5-6 well-greased ramekins; top with half the grated cheese and divide the crabmeat between the dishes.

Combine chopped onions with sour cream, mayonnaise and sherry; season to taste with salt, pepper and nutmeg. Spoon over the crabmeat in each dish and scatter the remaining grated cheese with the breadcrumbs over the top.

Drizzle melted butter over each and bake, uncovered, in a moderate oven for 25-30 minutes. Garnish each dish with lemon and parsley and serve hot.

Wine suggestion: The flavours in this crabmeat entrée would best be complemented by a white wine of hock style, light and delicate but with a crisp clean finish.

Crab Claws with Mayonnaise Aurore, recipe on page 26.

CRAB CLAWS WITH MAYONNAISE AURORE

SAUCE:

60 g (2 oz) butter
2 small white onions, finely chopped
2 teaspoons anchovy sauce
2 tablespoons tomato paste
½ cup dry vermouth
yolks of 4 hard-cooked eggs
1 cup egg mayonnaise

CRAB:

5-6 large crab claws
¼ cup white wine vinegar
¼ cup olive oil
1 clove garlic, crushed
salt and pepper
chive or parsley garnish

Heat the butter in a small saucepan; add onions and cook over low heat until softened but not browned. Add the anchovy sauce, tomato paste and vermouth and bring to the boil; cook for a few minutes to reduce the liquid by evaporation.

Allow to cool, add egg yolks and purée in an electric blender until smooth. Add to the mayonnaise; blend thoroughly, cover and refrigerate for 1-2 hours. Meanwhile, crack shells of crab claws and loosen meat inside for easy removal. Combine the next 5 ingredients together and drizzle into the cracks in the crab shells. Cover and refrigerate for 1-2 hours.

To serve: Three parts fill a large bowl with ice (crushed or cubes). Spoon the mayonnaise into a small bowl and place in the centre; arrange crab claws around. Provide lemon-water in finger bowls for each person.

Note: Large prawns or lobster pieces could replace the crab claws if desired.

Wine suggestion: This shellfish appetizer could be served with a glass of dry vermouth or, better still, an icy cold champagne, brut or dry to suit the taste.

SNAPPER AMBASSADOR

5-6 small snapper, bream or other fish
125 g (4 oz) unsalted butter, softened
2 tablespoons chopped fresh parsley
2 tablespoons chopped shallot or spring onion
2 teaspoons curry powder
1 teaspoon salt
¼ teaspoon pepper
2 small onions, skinned
3-4 cloves
1 bay leaf, broken
2 sprigs fresh dill
1½ cups white wine
1 cup water
1½ cups cream
3 egg yolks
1½ cups shredded Swiss cheese
paprika
salt and pepper
cucumber
salad dressing

Trim fish and carefully remove backbones by loosening the flesh from either side of the bone and severing it at either end.

Cream butter with parsley, shallot, curry powder, salt and pepper. Spread a portion into the insides of each of the fish and press together firmly; arrange in well-greased shallow ovenproof casseroles. Scatter the sliced onions, cloves, bay leaf and pieces of dill over the fish and pour the combined wine and water over and around. Cover loosely and poach in a moderate oven, basting occasionally, for 25-30 minutes.

Carefully transfer the fish to heated platter and strain the pan liquids into a saucepan. Bring to the boil, boil briskly until the liquid has reduced to about ½ cup. Lower heat and stir in cream, previously scalded and beaten with egg yolks. Stir until just commencing to boil, then spoon over each of the fish. Sprinkle equal portions of shredded cheese along each fish, sprinkle with paprika, salt and pepper and quickly glaze under a heated grill. Serve hot with a garnish of thinly sliced cucumber in salad dressing at each fish head.

Wine suggestion: A white burgundy or chablis with some bottle age would provide sufficient flavour to harmonize with this savoury seafood special.

PRAWNS FRANCOISE

15-18 large fresh prawns
2 cups white wine
12-15 oysters
60 g (2 oz) butter or substitute
½ cup finely chopped shallots or spring onions
¼ cup finely chopped red capsicum
1½ cups soft white breadcrumbs
2 teaspoons aniseed flavoured liqueur
2 eggs, beaten
salt and pepper
1 tablespoon chopped fresh dill
melted butter
dried breadcrumbs
paprika

Remove shells from prawns, leaving the tails intact; place in a saucepan with the wine and heat for a few minutes only. Lift away from heat and allow to cool; this will partially cook the prawns, making them easier to handle. Drain the prawns, remove the veins and cut lengthwise in halves to the tail section; open out and flatten slightly.

Add the oysters to the wine, reheat until they firm and the edges curl slightly; drain and cool, then chop finely. Boil the wine briskly to reduce the liquid by evaporation to approx. ⅓ cup; cool.

Heat butter in a pan, add shallots and capsicum and cook until softened. Add breadcrumbs, oysters and reduced wine with the liqueur and mix well. Gradually beat in eggs and season well with salt, pepper and dill. Simmer 5 minutes, stirring occasionally; allow to cool.

Arrange the prawns, cut side up, in a well greased scone tray; press a spoonful of oyster mixture onto each prawn and mound evenly. Brush melted butter over each prawn, sprinkle breadcrumbs over and lightly colour with paprika. Bake in a moderately hot oven for 10-12 minutes; lift out and serve hot.

Wine suggestion: This seafood savoury would taste particularly pleasant if accompanied by a Rhine Riesling wine with full fruit flavour. Aniseed flavoured liqueur such as Pernod, Anise or Sambuca for cooking.

PRAWNS WITH SAUCE ALMONDINE

1 kg (2 lb) small fresh uncooked prawns
2 teaspoons salt
1½ cups water
1 onion, quartered
1 teaspoon pickling spices
1 cup milk
½ cup dry sherry
4 thick slices white bread, crusts removed
90 g (3 oz) butter or substitute
extra 2 onions, chopped
¼ teaspoon pepper
1 teaspoon paprika
½ cup olive oil
1 cup finely ground almond meal
chopped fresh dill or parsley

Place the rinsed prawns in a saucepan with salt, water, quartered onion and pickling spices; bring to the boil and simmer for 3-4 minutes. Allow to cool in the liquid sufficiently for easy handling; lift out the prawns with a slotted spoon and reduce the pan liquids to 1 cup by boiling briskly; strain.

Peel prawns, devein and set aside. Sprinkle the combined milk and sherry over the bread slices; allow to soak in, then mash until smooth. Heat butter in a saucepan, add the extra onions, pepper and paprika and sauté until onions are softened, stirring frequently. Beat the bread mixture and the strained stock through the onions, cook for 5 minutes. Add the oil in a slow steady stream, whisking continuously; stir in the almond meal and prawns and heat through. Serve hot with a garnish of chopped fresh dill or parsley.

Wine suggestion: The slightly bland, sweet flavour of the almonds in this entrée would be complemented by a slightly sweet white wine, a Frontignan or moselle.

SEAFOOD FONDUE CRÊPES

CRÊPES

1 cup plain flour
½ teaspoon salt
pinch cayenne
3 eggs, separated
½ cup white wine
1 tablespoon melted butter
extra butter

FONDUE

¾ cup white wine
30 g (1 oz) butter
2 cups shredded Swiss cheese
1 tablespoon cornflour
2 tablespoons brandy
1½ cups flaked cooked fish or shellfish
salt and pepper

SAUCE

2 egg yolks
1 cup egg mayonnaise
90 g (3 oz) butter
1 tablespoon lemon juice
2 tablespoons cream

Sift flour, salt and cayenne into a bowl, whisk in the combined egg yolks, wine and melted butter; mix until batter is smooth. Fold in the lightly beaten egg whites and set aside for 30 minutes. Make crêpes as desired, using extra butter for pan greasing; set aside.

Combine the wine and butter in a saucepan, heat until simmering. Lower the heat and gradually fold in the combined cheese and cornflour; cook, stirring constantly, until the cheese has melted and blended through. Fold in the brandy and seafood, season well and keep warm.

Combine the egg yolks and mayonnaise in the top half of a double saucepan; cook over hot water until well warmed through. Gradually whisk in pieces of the butter until all is melted and blended through. Stir in the lemon juice and cream and keep warm.

To assemble: Spoon 2 tablespoons seafood fondue onto each crêpe and roll up; arrange in a greased casserole dish. Place in a moderate oven covered with aluminium foil to heat through 5-6 minutes.

Spoon the sauce over the crêpes and glaze quickly under a heated griller until lightly browned. Serve at once.

Wine suggestion: The rich cheese filling in this crêpe entrée would be enhanced by a dry white wine, perhaps one made from Semillon or Traminer grapes, served cold.

DEEP SEA MULLET CASSEROLE

2 large deep sea mullet
1 lemon
salt and pepper
flour
2 tablespoons vegetable oil
2 white onions, sliced
1 clove garlic, crushed
2-3 tomatoes, skinned and sliced
1 cup white wine
60 g (2 oz) butter or substitute
1 cup coarse white breadcrumbs
2 tablespoons capers
lemon and parsley

Remove head and skin from the mullet, scrape the flesh lightly with the back of a knife to remove excess oil. Cut the fish into thick steaks; use fish trimmings for stock if desired. Rub the fish with lemon juice, salt and pepper and coat with flour; fry in heated oil to brown lightly on both sides. Transfer fish steak to a greased large casserole, placing side by side.

Lightly fry onion slices and garlic in the pan; remove and arrange over the fish and cover with a layer of sliced tomatoes. Swill out the pan with the wine, then pour liquid over and around the tomatoes. Heat butter, add breadcrumbs and capers and toss; scatter over tomatoes. Cover with aluminium foil and bake in a moderate oven for 30-35 minutes. Serve hot, garnished with lemon and parsley.

Wine suggestion: A full flavoured white burgundy style made from Trebbiano or Chardonnay grapes would have sufficient character to complement the full 'fishy' flavour of the mullet.

Duckling in Red Wine, recipe on page 38.

PRAWNS FRANCINE

1 kg (2 lb) fresh uncooked prawns, shelled but
   tails intact
60 g (2 oz) butter or substitute
2 tablespoons vegetable oil
4-5 small onions, chopped
1 teaspoon curry powder
½ teaspoon salt
¼ teaspoon pepper
¾ cup white wine
¼ cup brandy
hot crusty bread

Rinse and devein the prawns as required. Heat butter and oil in a large frying pan, add chopped onions and curry powder and fry until onions are transparent.

Add prawns to the pan, scatter salt and pepper over and cook, turning frequently, until prawns are pink in colour. Pour the wine and brandy over, quickly cover to smother the aroma through the prawns, and simmer for a few minutes.

Spoon into well-heated bowls and serve with plenty of crusty bread slices.

Wine suggestion: Look for a white wine with an aromatic bouquet and slightly acid finish – such as a Blanquette or a Verdelhao varietal – to provide sufficient 'background' for these tasty prawns.

FISH QUENELLES ELEGANTE

1 cup white wine
2 cups water
1 onion, skinned
1 bay leaf, broken
2 sprigs parsley
1 teaspoon salt
6-8 peppercorns
500 g (1 lb) boned fish fillets, skinned
½ cup milk
125 g (4 oz) butter or substitute
1 cup flour
6 eggs
salted water (extra)

SAUCE

60 g (2 oz) butter or substitute
2-3 shallots or spring onions
2 tablespoons chopped parsley
4 tablespoons tomato purée
1 tablespoon aniseed flavoured liqueur
1-1½ cups small shelled prawns, deveined
1½ cups fish stock, strained
1 tablespoon cornflour
¼ cup white wine
salt and cayenne pepper
parsley sprigs

Combine the white wine, water, sliced onion, bay leaf, parsley sprigs, salt and peppercorns in a large shallow flameproof casserole. Place the fish fillets in the liquid, cover and poach in a moderate oven for 10 minutes only, until the fillets are firm. Remove fillets, drain and cool; chop or mince very finely, mash well.

Strain off ½ cup stock and add it to the milk in a saucepan; add half the butter and heat until bubbling. Remove from heat, add the flour all at once and beat until smooth. Return to heat and cook, stirring rapidly, until the mixture forms a ball, leaving the sides of the saucepan.

Remove from heat, turn into a basin and beat in 4 eggs one at a time, beating well after each addition. Add the minced fish, beat thoroughly, then beat in the remaining eggs and butter (softened). Spread mixture onto large platter and cool; chill well.

Shape the fish mixture into small oval croquettes on a lightly floured board, using two tablespoons and floured hands. Add extra water to the remaining stock in the casserole to form a depth of 5 cm (2 in); heat until simmering. Carefully lower the quenelles into the heated liquid; poach, uncovered, for 15-20 minutes, turning once. Lift quenelles with a slotted spoon onto a greased platter covered with absorbent paper, to drain.

Sauce: Heat the butter in a pan, add the chopped shallots and sauté until softened, stir in the parsley, tomato purée, liqueur, prawns and stock (made by reducing the casserole liquid by boiling briskly). Simmer over low heat for 10-15 minutes to blend all flavours.

Thicken as required with cornflour blended in the white wine; season to taste. To serve, spoon the sauce over heated quenelles on individual heated plates. Garnish with parsley.

Wine suggestion: Aniseed flavoured liqueur such as Pernod or Anisette, for the sauce. Choose a young fresh chablis, preferably from one of the cooler regions, to serve with this dish.

CHILLED SALMON MOUSSE

2 tablespoons gelatine
¼ cup boiling water
½ cup white wine
1 cup egg mayonnaise
1 tablespoon lemon juice
2 gherkins, chopped
1 teaspoon salt
¼ teaspoon cayenne pepper
3 x 220 g (7 oz) cans red salmon
1 small cucumber
1 stalk celery
1 lemon
lettuce for garnish
salad garnishes

Dissolve gelatine in boiling water, add wine and set aside. Combine the mayonnaise, lemon juice, gherkins, salt and cayenne. Open the salmon, remove skin and bones and flake; add to the mayonnaise. Peel and seed the cucumber and chop finely; chop the celery and add to the mayonnaise with the cucumber, mixing well.

Fold the gelatine liquid through the salmon mayonnaise, mixing thoroughly. Spoon into a well-oiled mould and chill until set. Unmould onto a serving platter, carefully remove any oil from the surface with a moistened tissue and brush lightly with diluted lemon juice.

Garnish with lettuce and salad vegetables as desired.

Wine suggestions: A moselle style wine, preferably with full fruit flavour but not too sweet, such as those from the cooler climates, would give the ideal balance for this popular summertime mousse.

TROUT ALEXANDER

5-6 trout, single serving size, backbones
  removed
1½ cups milk
½ cup water
2 teaspoons salt
5-6 peppercorns
2 bay leaves, broken
250 g (8 oz) button mushrooms
125 g (4 oz) butter or substitute
4-5 shallots or spring onions
1 cup shelled cooked small prawns
1½ cups cream
2 tablespoons cornflour
⅓ cup dry sherry
chopped parsley for garnish
lemon slices for garnish

Arrange the trimmed trout in a well-greased baking dish; pour combined milk and water over, sprinkle with salt, peppercorns and bay leaves. Cover loosely with aluminium foil and poach over moderate heat until fish flakes when tested with a fork. Transfer fish to heated serving platter and keep warm; reduce pan liquid by boiling briskly, strain and reserve 1 cup.

Sauté the whole or halved mushrooms in heated butter for 2-3 minutes; add chopped shallots and cook a further few minutes.

Stir in reserved fish stock, prawns and cream and heat slowly until almost boiling, simmer 5 minutes. Blend cornflour with sherry and stir into mushroom mixture; continue stirring over low heat for 1-2 minutes.

Spoon sauce over each trout and glaze quickly under a heated griller. Sprinkle parsley over and garnish with lemon slices; serve hot.

Wine suggestion: The distinctive flavour of the trout with the sherry sauce would be perfectly matched by a Traminer varietal wine, aromatic and spicy.

Main Course Meats and Poultry

CHICKEN MOUTARDE

2 x 1.5 kg (3 lb) chickens
4 tablespoons flour
salt and pepper
mustard
5-6 small onions, thickly sliced
2 tablespoons vegetable oil
60 g (2 oz) butter or substitute
125 g (4 oz) bacon rashers
2 cups chicken stock
1 cup white wine
1 sprig each parsley and thyme
2 bay leaves
1 cup cream
freshly chopped parsley

Cut chickens into serving sized pieces, removing as many of the cavity bones as possible; use these for making the stock. Combine flour with plenty of salt, pepper and mustard and rub this well into the surface of the chicken pieces. Sauté onions in heated oil and butter until just golden; remove and keep warm. Remove rinds from bacon and cut into 3-4 pieces; sauté in the heated oil until the fat is transparent; remove and place with the onions. Add chicken pieces to pan and sauté, turning frequently to brown all sides. Return onions and bacon and pour chicken stock and wine over.

Add parsley, thyme and bay leaves to pan, cover tightly and simmer gently for 1¼-1½ hours, until chicken is tender. Lift chicken pieces, onions and bacon onto a heated ovenproof dish, place in a moderately slow oven to keep hot; discard the parsley, thyme and bay leaves. Heat pan juices until boiling, stir well to loosen pan sediments. Combine any remaining seasoned flour with the cream and swirl into the liquid in the pan; reduce heat and adjust seasonings as required. Simmer without reboiling for 2-3 minutes, then pour over chicken pieces. Garnish with chopped parsley just before serving; add vegetables as desired.

Wine suggestion: A dry white wine of the riesling style, made from Semillon or Rhine Riesling grapes, would complement this light chicken dish.

LAMB NOISETTES WITH OLIVES

10-12 thick shortloin chops
1 tablespoon vegetable oil
2 tablespoons melted butter
salt and pepper
4-5 shallots or spring onions
2 lamb kidneys, skinned
1 tablespoon flour
¼ cup dry vermouth
1 clove garlic, crushed
1½ cups rich brown sauce
½ cup sliced stuffed olives

Remove bones and trim the lamb chops, form into rounds and secure with wooden picks, making noisettes. Heat oil and butter in a frying pan, add noisettes and fry on both sides to brown well. Transfer to a platter, remove the picks and season well.

Slice the shallots and kidneys, add to the pan and sauté, turning constantly for 1-2 minutes; sprinkle the flour over, stir through and cook a further minute. Add vermouth with garlic, spoon the sauce over and bring to bubbling point, stirring well. Return noisettes to the pan, scatter olives over and heat through over low heat. Serve hot with vegetables.

Wine suggestion: A dry red wine, full in flavour with a touch of tannin, will have sufficient character to complement the savoury sauce.

Pork Loin 'Sandwich' with Apple Raisin Stuffing, recipe on page 34.

TURKEY STRIPS L'ORANGE

1 kg (2 lb) uncooked turkey breast meat
½ cup flour
1 teaspoon salt
1 teaspoon paprika
¼ teaspoon pepper
125 g (4 oz) butter or substitute
2 tablespoons vegetable oil
¼ cup brandy and orange flavoured liqueur,
    mixed
¾ cup orange juice
¼ cup lemon juice
½ cup white wine
½ cup slivered almonds, browned
cooked noodles, butter
1 orange

Cut turkey meat into thin strips, toss in combined flour, salt, paprika and pepper to coat well; reserve excess flour. Heat half the butter and oil in a frying pan, add half the turkey strips and sauté, turning frequently, until lightly browned; remove and set aside.

Add remaining butter and oil, heat, add remaining turkey strips and repeat the browning process; return the first batch of strips, heating through. Warm the brandy-liqueur mixture, ignite and carefully pour over the turkey strips. Let flame briefly, then pour in the combined orange and lemon juices and heat through. Blend reserved flour with wine and add to the turkey mixture, stirring through. Cover and simmer for 10-15 minutes, until turkey pieces are tender.

Add the almonds, stir well and spoon over hot buttered noodles on a large platter. Cut very thin slices of orange rind, slice into fine strips and scatter over the turkey. Serve hot.

Wine suggestion: An orange flavoured liqueur such as Curaçao or Grand Marnier for cooking. A white wine made from the Chardonnay grape would add a little acid to counteract a too-sweet orange taste. Serve a similar wine, chilled.

PORK LOIN 'SANDWICH' WITH APPLE RAISIN STUFFING

5-6 very thick pork loin chops
½ cup rosé wine
2 tablespoons flour
1 tablespoon brown sugar
1 teaspoon mustard
60 g (2 oz) lard or bacon drippings
1 large onion, chopped
1-2 stalks celery, chopped
2 green apples, cored and diced
2 cups raisins
2½ cups soft bread cubes
1 teaspoon salt
¼ teaspoon pepper
2 tablespoons chopped fresh parsley
extra rosé wine

Trim the chops as required, slashing the skin along the back at intervals, arrange on a platter and brush generously with wine. Allow to stand 15 minutes; turn, brush the other side and stand again.

Drain chops, coat each side with a mixture of flour, brown sugar and mustard, patting on firmly; reserve the wine and juices. Brown chops lightly on both sides in heated lard in a large frying pan; lift out and set aside. Add chopped onion to the pan and fry until softened; add chopped celery and apples and cook a further 1-2 minutes; drain off any surplus fat. Mix in raisins, bread cubes, salt, pepper and parsley and moisten with about half the reserved wine liquid.

Prepare a large square of double thickness aluminium foil, grease the surface well and place a pork chop slightly to one side of the centre, rind side uppermost. Alternate portions of the stuffing and chops in a row, inserting 2-3 long skewers through the centre to hold intact. Lift up the foil and fold around the lower third of the chops to form a firm container.

Lift into a baking dish, brush remaining wine liquid over the top of the chops and cook in a moderately slow oven for 1¼-1½ hours. Loosen the foil from around the chops slightly, increase oven heat to hot and cook the meat a further 10-15 minutes to slightly brown and crispen the outsides. Carefully lift meat onto a heated platter and drain the juices in the foil into a small pan. Add extra wine as required to boil and form a gravy.

Serve the meat with vegetables as desired, accompanied by the wine gravy in a sauce boat.

Wine suggestion: A rosé or a light claret style wine with slight tannin astringency would make ideal partners for the pork.

FAMILY BEEF WITH ORANGE DUMPLINGS

3-4 rashers bacon, rind removed
1 kg (2 lb) stewing steak, chuck or blade
salt and pepper
flour
5-6 small white onions
1½ cups red wine
⅓ cup brandy
1 sprig each parsley and thyme
3 strips orange peel
1 large onion
4-5 cloves
1 cup beef stock, well seasoned
8-10 small mushroom cups
1 x 440 g (14 oz) can small whole carrots
chopped parsley

ORANGE DUMPLINGS

2 cups cooked mashed potatoes
salt and pepper
2-3 teaspoons grated orange rind
2 eggs
1 cup self raising flour
water – salted
melted butter or substitute

Cut bacon rashers into 3-4 pieces; cut the meat into large chunks. Toss meat in salt, pepper and flour, rubbing well into all sides. Fry bacon pieces in a large saucepan until crisp; remove and set aside.

Fry onions until browned all over; set aside. Add meat to pan and brown, turning constantly. Pour red wine and brandy over meat and cook 1-2 minutes at high heat to evaporate the alcohol. Add parsley and thyme sprigs, orange strips and onion stuck with cloves. Pour beef stock over, stir carefully and heat until bubbling; lower heat, cover and simmer gently 1½-1¾ hours.

Remove from heat, allow to stand 1 hour, then reheat slowly. Add the mushrooms, drained carrots, browned onions and bacon pieces, re-cover and simmer a further 30-45 minutes.

Orange Dumplings: Combine hot mashed potatoes with salt, pepper and orange rind to taste; beat in eggs one at a time and fold in sifted flour. Heat water to simmering point in a large saucepan, carefully drop in mounded dessertspoons of potato mixture and allow to poach, covered, for 10-12 minutes. Lift out with slotted spoon, toss in melted butter.

For serving: Turn beef stew into a large heated dish, removing parsley and thyme sprigs and clove-pierced onion. Sprinkle parsley over and arrange the orange dumplings around the edges. Serve hot.

Wine suggestion: This is an opportunity to serve a big red wine, a burgundy style, preferably made from Cabernet Sauvignon grapes from colder regions where vintage is late.

CRUMBED VEAL WITH CHESTNUT SAUCE

5-6 veal fillet steaks, cut 1 cm (½ inch) thick
flour
salt and pepper
1 egg
2 tablespoons evaporated milk
½ cup soft white breadcrumbs
¾ cup almond meal
60 g (2 oz) butter or substitute
2 tablespoons vegetable oil
60 g (2 oz) shelled almonds, slivered
1 x 250 g (8 oz) can chestnut purée
   (unsweetened)
½ cup white wine
1 cup sour cream

Trim veal fillets as required, flatten slightly with a mallet. Coat meat on both sides with flour, well seasoned with salt and pepper; press on firmly. Combine beaten egg with milk, brush over meat to coat. Press into combined breadcrumbs and almond meal to coat firmly all over.

Heat butter and oil in a large pan; when foaming add crumbed meat and fry over moderate heat until golden brown on both sides and cooked through. Transfer meat to a heated platter and keep hot in a moderate oven.

Add the almonds to the pan and sauté until golden brown, remove and set aside, sprinkling with salt. Add the chestnut purée and wine to the pan and heat, stirring continuously, until bubbling. Lower the heat and gradually stir in sour cream; heat through without boiling and season to taste.

Serve the veal with chestnut sauce poured over; sprinkle salted almonds over each and add vegetables as desired.

Wine suggestion: A moselle style wine with slight sweetness and pronounced fruit flavour would suit those who prefer less acid wines; otherwise use a Traminer varietal wine to complement this dish. Serve chilled.

STEAK ROHAN

5-6 Scotch fillet steaks, cut 6 cm (2½ in) thick
30 g (1 oz) butter or substitute
2 tablespoons vegetable oil
3-4 tablespoons brandy
salt and pepper
3-4 small onions, sliced
2 tablespoons flour
extra 90 g (3 oz) butter or substitute
1 cup water
¾ cup madeira wine
1 teaspoon beef extract
2 teaspoons plum jam
2-3 gherkins, cut into strips
250 g (8 oz) button mushrooms sautéed in 90 g
   (3 oz) butter

MARINADE:

¼ cup madeira wine
¼ cup red wine vinegar
⅓ cup vegetable oil

Trim steak and flatten with a meat mallet to about 2.5 cm (1 in) thick. Combine marinade ingredients, mixing well; brush steak all over with the marinade and set aside for 1 hour , turning and brushing occasionally. Heat butter and vegetable oil in a large pan and brown steaks quickly on both sides to seal in the juices. Pour brandy over the steaks, allow to become warmed and ignite; when the flames die down transfer the steaks to an ovenproof casserole and sprinkle each with salt and pepper; keep hot in a moderate oven.

Toss onions in flour and add to frying pan with the extra butter; sauté, turning frequently, until lightly browned. Combine the water, wine, beef extract and plum jam and pour over onions; cook, stirring frequently, until bubbling. Reduce the heat and simmer for a few minutes, then add gherkins and lightly season with salt and pepper.

Spoon sauce over the steaks and return to the oven for 10-15 minutes. Arrange the mushrooms around the edge of the casserole and serve hot with vegetables as desired.

Wine suggestion: The madeira provides a distinctive rich taste for the beef; this would be complemented by serving a claret style wine with full fruit flavour.

Family Beef with Orange Dumplings, recipe on page 35.

DUCKLING IN RED WINE

1 large pork shoulder chop, approx. 250 g (½ lb)
60 g (2 oz) lard or bacon drippings
2-3 small ducklings
5-6 small onions
250 g (½ lb) small mushroom cups
2 cups rich chicken stock
1½ cups red wine
2 teaspoons French mustard
beurre manié (blended butter and flour)
salt and pepper
½-¾ cup green olives
chopped parsley

Remove bone from chop and cut meat into 2.5 cm (1 in) cubes; sauté in the heated lard in a large saucepan until well browned; lift out and set aside. Cut ducklings into serving sized sections removing as many of the cavity bones as possible, add to the pork fat and sauté, turning frequently, until browned all over; lift out and set aside. Add skinned whole onions to the pan and brown also; drain off any excess fat.

Return duckling pieces to the pan, add whole mushrooms and pour chicken stock over; bring slowly to the boil, stirring occasionally. Combine wine with mustard and pour into the pan; cover, reduce heat and allow to simmer for 1½-2 hours until the duckling is tender; do not overcook.

Lift duckling pieces out of pan and keep hot while thickening the liquid with small quantities of beurre manié stirred through; return the cooked pork cubes. Taste for additional salt and pepper if required and stir in pitted olives. Return the duckling, reheat as required and garnish with chopped parsley just before serving.

Wine suggestion: Young ducklings with no strong gamey flavour would be best served with a light red wine, one made from straight Shiraz grapes.

HAM ROLLS WITH VEAL STUFFING

500 g (1 lb) finely minced veal
1 cup cream cheese
½ cup finely chopped shallots or spring onions
1 teaspoon salt
¼ teaspoon pepper
pinch nutmeg
cream
10-12 thin slices ham from a boned roll
butter or substitute
2 cups madeira wine
1 tablespoon brandy

SAUCE:

stock – from above
3 cups sliced button mushrooms
salt and pepper
¾ cup cream
1 tablespoon cornflour

Combine veal with cream cheese, chopped shallots and seasonings. Mix together thoroughly, adding sufficient cream to hold mixture together. Spoon equal portions of the stuffing onto each ham slice; roll up and secure with string or thread. Heat butter in a flameproof casserole to generously cover the base; add ham rolls and fry, turning frequently, until lightly browned. Pour wine and brandy over and around the rolls; cover tightly and simmer over very low heat for 40-45 minutes to cook the veal stuffing. Lift the ham rolls onto a platter and keep hot. Reduce pan liquid to about 1½ cups by boiling briskly and use as stock for the sauce.

Sauce: Add sliced mushrooms to stock in casserole and simmer for 5 minutes, covered. Sprinkle in salt and pepper to season well. Blend cream with cornflour, slowly swirl into the mushroom mixture, stir constantly until thickened and smooth. Serve spooned over the ham rolls with cooked noodles, rice or creamed potatoes as desired.

Wine suggestion: Search for a fruity madeira with a dry finish for use in the recipe. Serve a full flavoured white burgundy, made from Chardonnay or Trebbiano grapes, with the meal.

STUFFED BEEF POT ROAST

2 kg (4 lb) buttock steak in one large square
  piece
2-3 tablespoons bacon drippings
2 brown onions, chopped
2 small carrots, diced
125 g (4 oz) open flat mushrooms
2 slices white bread soaked in ¼ cup red wine
1 tablespoon chopped parsley
1 egg
seasoned salt and pepper
1 cup rich brown stock
1 cup red wine (extra)
1 x 440 g (14 oz) can tomatoes
beurre manié (blended butter and flour)

Brown all sides of the buttock steak in heated drippings in a large saucepan; lift out and allow to cool. Cut a thick slice from the top of the meat; with a sharp knife hollow out the centre to within 2.5 cm (1 in) of the sides and base; mince the removed meat finely. Add the onions and carrots to the pan and fry until browned with the minced meat.

Chop mushrooms coarsely and add to the mince mixture with the mashed, soaked bread, parsley and beaten egg. Season well and mix thoroughly; fill into the centre of the meat joint, replace the 'lid' and tie with string. Return to saucepan, pour stock, wine and tomatoes with their juice over; cover tightly and simmer slowly for 2-2½ hours. Lift meat onto a platter, remove string. Thicken the pan juices with small pieces blended butter and flour; season well. Serve the meat cut in thick slices with the sauce poured over and vegetables as desired.

Wine suggestion: This seasoned beef pot roast has sufficient flavour to warrant a good 'gutsy' red wine, one with a little age.

ROLLED VEAL WITH SAGE

1 large shoulder veal, bone removed
1 thick slice ham steak
4-5 spring onions or shallots
1½ cups soft white breadcrumbs
8-10 fresh sage leaves
salt and pepper
1 egg, beaten
2-3 tablespoons oil
2 stalks celery
2 white onions
1 cup white wine
½ cup sour cream or evaporated milk

Spread the veal shoulder out on a board as flat as possible, skin side down. Dice ham finely and fry over low heat until the fat is transparent; add diced spring onions, fry a minute longer. Mix in breadcrumbs, coarsely chopped sage, salt and pepper as desired and bind together with the egg. Spread over veal, roll up and skewer or tie securely; rub a little salt and pepper into the skin.

Heat oil in a large baking dish, add veal and lightly brown all over; remove. Add coarsely chopped celery and onion to the dish; heat to brown lightly, season. Replace veal on top of the vegetables, pour wine over and cover loosely with aluminium foil.

Cook in a moderate oven for 1 hour, remove foil and baste meat with vegetables and pan juices. Cook a further 1-1½ hours, basting meat from time to time; gradually reduce oven heat if required. Lift meat onto a platter and keep warm.

Strain the vegetables from pan juices and boil the juices over high heat, stirring to loosen any sediment, until reduced to about 1 cup in quantity. Lower the heat, add sour cream and swirl in; season to taste.

Cut the veal into slices and serve on warmed plates with vegetables as desired. Spoon a little sauce over meat slices and serve remainder in a sauce boat.

Wine suggestion: Veal, though soft in flavour, has a richness which goes well with a white burgundy style wine made from Chardonnay grapes.

GLAZED GOOSE WITH CRUSTED SEASONING SQUARES

1 medium goose, approx. 4 kg (8 lb)
2 onions, quartered
1 green apple, cored and quartered
salt and pepper
½ cup brandy
2 tablespoons wine vinegar
2 tablespoons honey
1 tablespoon soy sauce
1 tablespoon chopped fresh sage
½ teaspoon onion salt
½ cup red currant or apple jelly
extra brandy

SEASONING:

3 cups small bread cubes
1 onion and 1 apple, finely chopped
1 teaspoon salt
¼ teaspoon pepper
1 tablespoon chopped fresh sage
250 g (8 oz) bacon rashers, finely chopped
1 egg
2 tablespoons brandy-honey marinade

Trim the goose as required, cleaning the body cavity thoroughly. Quarter the onions and apple and place in the cavity; sprinkle in some salt and pepper and truss or skewer to retain shape. Combine the following 7 ingredients, warming slightly to dissolve the honey and jelly. Prick surface of goose all over with tip of a sharp knife; brush the marinade all over and set aside for 2 hours, brushing the bird frequently. Place goose on its side on a roasting rack in a baking dish and roast in a moderately slow oven for ½ hour. Turn the goose to the other side, brush again with marinade and roast a further ½ hour. Continue the turning, brushing process every ½ hour until a total of 3 hours has elapsed; test the leg joints and continue roasting as required. Remove goose to platter and keep hot.

Meanwhile prepare the seasoning by combining the bread cubes with the remaining ingredients. Press seasoning into a square cake pan and cook in the oven during the last hour or so of the roasting of the goose.

Drain off as much as possible of the fat from the baking dish, add the extra brandy, warm and ignite. Stir well to loosen pan sediment, season if required and strain into a sauce boat; keep hot.

Brush a little of the fat from the dish over the surface of the seasoning; cut into squares. Present the goose for carving with squares of the seasoning arranged around the dish. Serve sauce separately.

For Roast Duck: Replace the apple with orange and use parsley instead of sage. Adjust cooking times as required.

For Roast Turkey: Substitute celery and a sprig of marjoram for the apple and use extra marjoram in the marinade. Adjust cooking times as required.

Wine suggestion: Depending on the poultry used serve a full flavoured white burgundy or light claret made from a blend of Cabernet and Hermitage (Shiraz) grapes.

Cranberry Chutney, for poultry, recipe on page 52.

Vegetables and Salads

CABBAGE TOSS

1 small tight cabbage
125 g (4 oz) thick bacon rashers, rind removed
½ cup chopped onion
1 teaspoon caraway seeds
1 cup wine (see note)
pepper
butter

Shred the washed cabbage finely, discarding thick centre stems. Chop bacon into small pieces, place with onion in a flameproof casserole and cook over moderate heat until bacon is crisp and onions lightly browned. Add caraway seeds and salt and stir through. Add cabbage and toss well. Pour wine over, heat until steaming, then cover and place in a moderately hot oven. Cook for 30-35 minutes; cabbage should be still just slightly crisp. Remove from oven, sprinkle with plenty of pepper, dot with butter and toss well. Return to the oven uncovered, for a further few minutes. Drain if necessary and serve hot.

Note: If using white cabbage use white wine; for red cabbage, red wine.

Wine suggestion: The choice of meat with which this cabbage dish is to be served will govern the serving of an accompanying wine. A bulk white or red wine would suffice for cooking.

CRUMBED SPROUTS WITH PIQUANT SAUCE

500 g (1 lb) even sized Brussel sprouts
salted water
¾ cup dry vermouth
¼ cup finely chopped shallots or spring onions
1 cup egg mayonnaise
2 teaspoons horseradish
2 gherkins, chopped
2 eggs, beaten
seasoned salt and pepper
flour
dried white breadcrumbs
oil for frying

Remove outer leaves from sprouts, trim stalks and cut a cross slash into each stalk end to speed cooking. Boil in salted water for 5-7 minutes only, drain and plunge into cold water to prevent further cooking.

Combine the vermouth and shallots in a saucepan, bring to the boil and boil briskly to reduce liquid to ¼ cup. Remove from heat, cool and gradually stir into the mayonnaise; add horseradish and gherkins, cover and chill.

Drain the sprouts, dry well and brush lightly with beaten eggs, dip into the seasoned flour to coat, then brush again with the eggs. Toss in dried breadcrumbs, coating thoroughly. Deep fry in batches in heated oil until browned, drain on absorbent paper. Serve hot with the piquant sauce for spooning on side of plate.

Wine suggestion: Serve these interesting sprouts with a meat which does not contain wine in cooking so there are no conflicting tastes. Choice of wine depends on the meat.

MUSHROOMS IN WHITE PORT

500 g (1 lb) mushroom cups
125 g (4 oz) butter or substitute
1 cup white port wine or light muscat
salt and pepper

Wipe, trim and thinly slice the mushrooms. Heat the butter in a large pan and when foaming add the mushrooms. Cook over moderate heat, stirring occasionally, until mushrooms are softened and most of the juices in the pan have evaporated. Pour the wine over and continue cooking, stirring frequently, for 5-7 minutes. Increase heat for 1-2 minutes to evaporate more of the pan juices. Sprinkle salt and plenty of pepper over, stir through and serve at once.

Wine suggestion: The use of a white port with these mushrooms will give a slight sweetness but not effect the overall cream-brown colour. If served over lamb or beef, drink a light red wine.

GLAZED CARROTS IN SAUTERNES

500 g (1 lb) young carrots
125 g (4 oz) butter or substitute
¾ cup sauternes wine
½ cup water
1 teaspoon salt
2 tablespoons brown sugar
chopped parsley

Cut carrots into slices or strips; place in a saucepan with half the butter, ½ cup wine, water and salt. Bring quickly to the boil, cover tightly and cook on lowered heat for 10-15 minutes depending on size of carrot pieces. Drain off the liquid (reserve for stock), add sugar, remaining butter and wine and stir until butter has melted. Return to heat and finish cooking until carrots are almost tender, stirring or shaking the pan frequently. Add chopped parsley, toss through and serve hot.

Wine suggestion: As these sweet tasting carrots would probably accompany a mild or sweet tasting meat, suitable accompanying wines would be a chilled white burgundy or rosé or a light red wine.

SPINACH AND RICE IN MADEIRA WINE

2½ cups lightly cooked or frozen spinach
90 g (3 oz) butter or substitute
1 tablespoon flour
1½ cups cooked long grain rice
½ teaspoon salt
¼ teaspoon pepper
¼ teaspoon ground nutmeg
1 cup evaporated milk
¼ cup madeira wine
30 g (1 oz) butter (extra)

Drain, or thaw and drain spinach well. Heat butter in a frying pan, add spinach and heat through, tossing well to loosen the spinach. Sprinkle flour over and stir through, then fold in rice.

Combine salt, pepper and nutmeg with evaporated milk and wine; pour over the spinach and cook until just commencing to boil. Reduce heat and simmer for 2-3 minutes. Spear the extra butter on the point of a knife and pass over the surface of the spinach to melt and produce a glaze.

Serve hot with grilled or pan-fried lamb chops, sautéed chicken or crumbed veal.

Wine suggestion: The flavour of the madeira wine should be sufficiently distinctive to serve with a meat dish containing no wine. Choice of accompanying wine will depend upon the meat.

HERBED POTATOES

90 g (3 oz) butter or substitute
8-10 medium sized new potatoes
3 small onions, thinly sliced
1 clove garlic, crushed
2 tablespoons flour
1 teaspoon salt
¼ teaspoon pepper
½ cup chicken stock
½ cup white wine
1 tablespoon chopped fresh thyme
1 tablespoon chopped fresh parsley

Heat butter in a large saucepan, add scrubbed, thickly sliced potatoes and thinly sliced onions and fry, turning frequently until slightly browned. Add garlic, flour, salt and pepper and continue frying, turning constantly, a further minute. Pour combined stock and wine over, sprinkle with thyme and simmer, tightly covered, until liquid is absorbed and potatoes tender. Sprinkle in parsley and toss well just before serving. Serve with grilled or baked fish, sautéed or baked chicken or crumbed lamb cutlets.

Wine suggestion: Wine from a flagon or cask, perhaps a riesling style, would give a little extra flavour in cooking to this potato scallop. Accompanying wine will depend on accompanying meat.

BEETROOT IN PORT WINE SAUCE

15-18 very small beetroot
water
salt, peppercorns and cloves
1½ cups port wine
1 tablespoon sugar
2 tablespoons arrowroot or cornflour
60 g (2 oz) butter or substitute

Cut leaf tops to within 2.5 cm (1 in) of the beetroot and discard. Place vegetables in large saucepan with water to cover, 2 teaspoons salt, 1 teaspoon peppercorns and 5-6 cloves. Bring to the boil, cover and simmer for 15-20 minutes, until beetroot are just tender. Drain off the beetroot, strain liquid and reserve 1½ cups; slip skins from the beetroot. Cut into pieces if necessary.

Return the reserved liquid to saucepan, add wine and heat slowly with the sugar. Blend arrowroot with a little water, stir into the sauce and cook slowly until thickened. Swirl in the butter, add salt and pepper if required and return the beetroot to the pan. Heat thoroughly and serve.

Wine suggestion: Port wine teams well with the slightly sweet taste of beetroot in this unusual vegetable dish, ideal to serve with corned meats and a full fruity white burgundy wine.

OVEN TOASTED RICE

1 cup long grain rice
60 g (2 oz) butter or substitute
1 cup rich chicken stock
¾ cup white wine
½ cup chopped shallots or spring onions
1-2 tablespoons soy sauce
salt and pepper

Scatter rice into a baking dish and place in a moderate oven to toast lightly. Add butter, mix until melted and return to oven for 2-3 minutes. Carefully pour in heated stock and stir the wine through; cover and cook in the oven for 25 minutes. Loosen the rice with a fork, add shallots and soy sauce and toss through; season well. Return to oven to partially soften the shallots and evaporate any remaining liquid. Serve hot.

Wine suggestion: Use a white wine from a bottle, flagon or cask for cooking; the flavour should not affect the choice of wine to accompany the meat.

Vegetable Medley: Herbed Potatoes, recipe on page 44; Spinach and Rice in Madeira Wine, recipe on page 43; Crumbed Sprouts with Piquant Sauce, recipe on page 42.

ONIONS A LA GRECQUE

36-40 tiny white onions
water
½ cup olive oil
1-2 cloves garlic, sliced
1½ cups water
¾ cup white wine
4 tablespoons white vinegar
1 teaspoon salt
1 teaspoon mustard seeds, crushed
3-4 cloves, crushed
6-8 peppercorns, crushed
2 bay leaves, broken
1 cup sultanas
chopped basil or parsley

Drop onions into boiling water for 1-2 minutes, drain and remove the skins. Place in a large enamel-lined saucepan and add the following 10 ingredients. Add extra water or wine to cover the onions if necessary. Cover pan and bring to the boil, lower the heat and simmer for 10 minutes. Add the sultanas, stir well and allow onions and liquid to cool slowly. Turn into a glass or china bowl, cover and chill overnight. Drain onions into a bowl through a slotted spoon, sprinkle basil over and serve as a side accompaniment to hot or cold meat dishes.

Wine suggestion: These spicy pickled onions would be admirably suited to serve with full flavoured meat dishes: therefore, the choice of accompanying wine would probably be a good dry red.

TWO-CHEESE SALAD

1 cup sour cream
1 cup crumbled blue vein cheese
2 teaspoons French mustard
½ teaspoon cummin seed
2 tablespoons port wine
500 g (1 lb) mild cheese (Swiss or Edam)
lettuce cups
3 hard-boiled eggs
parsley

Combine sour cream with crumbled cheese, mustard, cummin and port wine; mix well, cover and chill overnight to allow the flavours to develop. Cut the mild cheese into matchstick slices and mix lightly into the cream-cheese dressing. Arrange lettuce cups in individual bowls, spoon equal portions of the cheese mixture into each. Garnish with quarters of shelled hard boiled egg and parsley. Serve as a light entrée or side salad as desired.

Wine suggestion: Serve this salad as an accompaniment to a grill or a similar meat cooked without wine; then look to the mild or stronger flavour of the meat for the choice of drinking wine.

WILTED LETTUCE-ONION SALAD

1 large firm lettuce
4 small white onions
½ cup vegetable oil
½ cup white wine
1 clove garlic, halved
pinch sugar
seasoned salt
Tabasco sauce
125 g (4 oz) Swiss cheese slices
1 cup fried bread croûtons
chopped parsley

Separate and wash the lettuce leaves; drain well and break into bite-sized pieces. Cut onions into thin rings; place in alternate layers with the lettuce in a bowl. Toss. Combine oil, white wine, garlic and sugar in a saucepan, season with salt and few drops Tabasco sauce. Heat until boiling, stirring occasionally; remove the garlic. Drizzle the hot dressing over the lettuce and onion rings; toss well. Cut the cheese slices into thin strips and scatter over the salad with bread croûtons. Garnish with parsley and serve.

Wine suggestion: A young, acid wine will give sufficient tang to the dressing for this salad but this would not affect the serving of a fresh white wine with the meal itself.

Sauces, Marinades and Dressings

CREAMED ONION SAUCE

6-8 large white onions
water
1½ cups chicken stock, well seasoned
1½ cups white wine
½ cup rice
¼ teaspoon nutmeg
1 cup cream
60g (2 oz) butter or substitute
salt and pepper

Thinly slice the onions and place in a saucepan, cover with water and bring quickly to the boil; simmer 1-2 minutes. Drain, cover with cold water and drain again; place in top half of a double saucepan. Add the chicken stock, wine, rice and nutmeg, cover and cook over boiling water until the onions are very tender, about 40 minutes.

Rub the mixture through a fine sieve and return to saucepan; reheat over hot water. Stir in cream and butter, add salt and pepper to taste and set aside, covered, until ready for use.

Wine suggestion: This strongly flavoured sauce would usually be used with a strong flavoured meat so that a full bodied white burgundy style wine made from Chardonnay grapes would be ideal.

WHITE WINE CHEESE SAUCE

60 g (2 oz) butter or substitute
1 tablespoon flour
2 cups white wine
1 cup rich chicken stock
2 cups grated mature Cheddar cheese
2 egg yolks
salt and cayenne pepper

Heat butter in a saucepan, add flour and blend well; lower heat. Stir in white wine and chicken stock, heating slowly until thickened and bubbling. Over very low heat, gradually whisk in small quantities of grated cheese, allowing each quantity to melt and blend through. Spoon a little of the sauce into the egg yolks to warm and blend, then return the mixture to the cheese sauce, whisking until smooth and foaming. Season to taste, cover and keep hot over hot water until ready for use.

Wine suggestion: This rich cheese sauce is fairly bland in flavour and would not dominate a white wine of the Clare Riesling variety – a soft wine with moderate acid content.

RED WINE SAUCE

¼ cup red currant jelly
1½ cups rich beef stock
¾ cup red wine
¼ cup tomato purée
¼ cup combined chopped fresh parsley and thyme
2 bay leaves, broken
½ teaspoon brown sugar
beurre manié (blended butter and flour)
salt and pepper
2 teaspoons lemon juice

Combine red currant jelly with the following 6 ingredients and bring to the boil. Cover and simmer for 15-20 minutes, strain through fine mesh and return to the saucepan. Thicken the liquid by gradually stirring in pieces of blended butter and flour; simmer a few minutes. Taste for extra seasoning as required and stir the lemon juice through.

Wine suggestion: A rich red sauce such as this needs a full bodied red wine with good oak character and tannin finish; a red wine from grapes grown in the colder regions would be an ideal choice.

NUTMEG WINE SAUCE

FOR POULTRY

pan drippings from roast chicken, duck or
   turkey
1 liver from chicken, duck or turkey
1 large onion, finely chopped
1 clove garlic, crushed
1 bay leaf, broken
1 teaspoon ground nutmeg
1 cup white wine
1 cup rich chicken stock
2-3 teaspoons lemon juice
salt and pepper
½ cup sour cream

Carefully skim as much fat as possible from the pan drippings, scrape surface to loosen pieces. Chop the rinsed liver finely and add to the drippings with onion; cook, stirring constantly, until liver is browned and onion softened. Add garlic, bay leaf and nutmeg; pour wine and chicken stock over and heat, stirring occasionally, until boiling; simmer 5 minutes. Add lemon juice and seasonings to taste; strain through fine mesh into a saucepan and heat through. Swirl in sour cream and allow to heat without boiling. Pour into a heated sauce boat and serve.

Wine suggestion: A white wine of the fuller white burgundy style is used in this recipe for colour reasons but perhaps a light red wine might better complement the chosen meat.

PROVENCALE SAUCE

60 g (2 oz) butter or substitute
2 onions, thinly sliced
1 green capsicum, thinly sliced
3-4 tomatoes, skinned and chopped
8-10 green olives, stoned and chopped
4-5 large flat mushrooms, chopped
bouquet garni (tied parsley, thyme
   and bayleaf)
1 clove garlic, bruised
few whole cloves
sugar
1 cup red wine
salt and pepper

Heat butter in a saucepan, add onions and capsicum and cook for 3-4 minutes over medium heat, stirring frequently. Add chopped tomatoes, olives and mushrooms with the bouquet garni, garlic, cloves and a pinch of sugar. Pour the red wine over, bring to the boil, then cover and simmer for 25-30 minutes.

Discard the bouquet garni, garlic and cloves, and season to taste with salt and pepper; stir well. Simmer 1-2 minutes.

Wine suggestions: Depending on the meat served with this sauce, choose a red wine made from Cabernet Sauvignon or blended Cabernet and Shiraz grapes, with lightness or fuller body according to taste.

BRANDIED APRICOT SAUCE

FOR POULTRY AND GAME

250 g (8 oz) dried apricots
2 cups warm water
1 lemon
¼ teaspoon salt
1 teaspoon ground ginger
½ teaspoon mixed spice
½ cup brown sugar
½ cup sweet sherry
½ cup toasted almonds or pine nuts
1-2 tablespoons brandy

Cover apricots with warm water and set aside overnight to soften. Transfer to a saucepan and add 3-4 strips lemon peel, 2 tablespoons lemon juice and the salt, ginger, spice, brown sugar and sherry. Bring slowly to the boil and simmer gently for 15 minutes; cool slightly and press through a sieve or blend to form a purée. Just before serving fold in the chopped nuts and add brandy to taste. Serve hot or cold as required.

Note: This sauce refrigerates and freezes well at the purée stage before the addition of the nuts and brandy.

Wine suggestion: This sweet yet spicy fruit sauce would be complemented by a light claret style red wine, or for those who prefer it, a chilled rosé.

Provencale Sauce, recipe on page 48.

DESSERT CHEESE SAUCE

1 tablespoon cornflour
2 tablespoons water
¾ cup syrup from preserved fruits in liqueur, apricots, peaches or cherries
½ cup cream
1¼ cups shredded mild Swiss cheese
pinch nutmeg

Blend cornflour with water, add to fruit syrup in a saucepan and heat, stirring constantly, until thickened. Stir in cream, lower heat and simmer 1 minute. Remove from heat, gradually add the cheese, stirring until melted and blended through. Flavour with nutmeg to taste and serve with the preserved fruits.

Note: If not using fruits in liqueur, use syrup from canned fruits and add 1-2 tablespoons brandy or fruit liqueur according to fruit.

Wine suggestion: A chilled sauternes, a spätlese or an auslese wine would all give a degree of sweetness to complement this sauce, depending on choice of fruit and individual taste.

FOAMING BRANDY SAUCE

125 g (4 oz) butter, softened
1½ cups icing sugar
1 large egg, separated
pinch of salt
2 tablespoons brandy
¾ cup cream, chilled
nutmeg

Cream butter and gradually heat in sifted icing sugar. Beat in egg yolk and salt and turn into the top of a glass double saucepan. Cook over hot but not boiling water, whisking continuously until the mixture is light and very fluffy, 6-8 minutes. Remove from heat, add brandy and heat through; cool and chill. Beat egg white until stiff; beat cream until thickened then carefully fold the two together. Just before serving fold the cream mixture into the butter mixture, adding ground nutmeg to taste. Serve over steamed fruit puddings or baked fruit pies.

Wine suggestion: There should be sufficient strength of flavour in the pudding or pie with this sauce to stand up to the flavour of a full Traminer or Rhine Riesling.

WINE VINEGAR

4-5 litres (1 gallon) red or white wine
1 cup spaghetti
1 cup rice
thyme
parsley

Pour 4-5 litres (1 gallon) red or white wine in a large clean glass or porcelain crock; add 1 cup uncooked broken spaghetti and 1 cup uncooked rice. Cover with a cheesecloth or fine netting and store in a cool dark place for 2 months. Scoop off amounts of vinegar required for bottling and replenish liquid in the crock with additional wine.

Add thyme, parsley, tarragon or other fresh herb sprigs to the bottled vinegar, seal tightly and set aside for a further week before use.

Wine suggestion: A bulk red or white wine from cask or flagon would be both economical and suitable for making wine vinegar.

WHITE WINE SALAD DRESSING

⅔ cup white wine
⅓ cup tarragon vinegar
1 egg
1 egg yolk
1 teaspoon French mixed mustard
¼ teaspoon English mixed mustard
½ teaspoon salt
¼ teaspoon white pepper
1 white onion
1½ cups olive oil

Combine the first 8 ingredients in a blender; add 2 teaspoons onion juice (made by scraping the sharp edge of a teaspoon across the cut surface of the onion) to the mixture.

Pour in about ½ cup of olive oil and blend for 10-15 seconds at high speed. Lift the lid of the blender and gradually pour in the remaining oil at a lower speed until all the oil has been absorbed into the dressing. Chill thoroughly, then reblend 2-3 seconds before use.

Blue Cheese Dressing: Add ½ cup crumbled blue vein cheese and 1 tablespoon brandy with the onion.

Sherried Egg Dressing: Add 2 extra egg yolks and drizzle in 2 tablespoons dry sherry with the oil.

Sour Cream Dressing: Reduce the white wine and oil by half and blend in 1 cup sour cream.

Wine suggestion: A fresh, high acid white wine would give a lift to the flavours in this dressing without dominating the wine used to accompany the food.

CREAM CHEESE FRUIT DRESSING

1 x 250 g (8 oz) packet cream cheese
2 tablespoons concentrated orange juice
pinch salt
1 tablespoon icing sugar
½ cup sweet sherry

Allow cream cheese to stand at room temperature to soften; mash with a fork and work in the orange juice. Flavour with salt and icing sugar and blend in the sweet sherry. Serve over tropical fruits.

Wine suggestion: Choice of wine for serving will depend on acidity of fresh fruits used, or personal taste. Perhaps a sparkling wine or sauternes.

MAYONNAISE PIQUANTE

1½ cups egg mayonnaise
2-3 anchovy fillets, finely chopped
10-12 capers
3-4 shallots or spring onions, chopped
2 tablespoons chopped fresh parsley
1 tablespoon chopped fresh chervil or tarragon
¼ cup white wine
2 teaspoons lemon juice
2 hard-cooked eggs, shelled and chopped

Combine mayonnaise with anchovies and capers; set aside.

Place shallots, parsley and chervil in a saucepan, add wine and lemon juice and bring to the boil, simmer 2-3 minutes and cool. Beat the wine mixture into the mayonnaise, fold in the chopped eggs and chill.

Additional flavourings, depending on use: horseradish cream, mixed mustard, curry paste, tomato paste, chilli sauce or chives.

Wine suggestion: The piquant flavour of this salad sauce would overpower the serving of a delicate wine so choose from the range of fresh, full flavoured whites or rosés.

VERSATILE WINE MARINADE

2-3 sprigs parsley
1 large onion
½ teaspoon salt
4-5 peppercorns, cracked
1 cup olive or vegetable oil
2 tablespoons wine vinegar, red or white
1 cup wine, red or white

Chop parsley (including stalks) and onion into small pieces; place with salt and pepper in a glass or china dish and crush together with a wooden spoon. Pour oil, vinegar and wine over, mix well and allow flavours to blend for 10-15 minutes before use.

Additions

For barbecue steaks, use red wine and add 1 table-spoon Worcestershire sauce, 2 tablespoons tomato chutney and 1 teaspoon mustard; garlic is optional.

For pan-fried steaks, use red wine and add 2-3 cloves, 1 bayleaf and a sprinkling of nutmeg to the parsley-onion mix.

For hogget or mutton, use white wine and add 2 sprigs rosemary, mint or thyme, 1 teaspoon sugar and a few juniper berries to the parsley-onion mix.

For older poultry or game, use red wine and add 5-6 juniper berries, 2 cloves garlic, 3-4 cloves and 2 tablespoons red currant jelly to the parsley-onion mix.

For sweet-sour pork, use white wine and add 1 tablespoon brown sugar, 2 tablespoons soy sauce and pineapple juice in place of the vinegar.

For seafoods, use white wine and add 2 teaspoons crushed root ginger, replacing the vinegar with dry sherry or Vermouth.

For saté sticks, use white wine with yoghurt and lemon juice in place of the vinegar; add 1 tablespoon mixed cumin, turmeric and ginger and a pinch of hot chilli. Add peanut butter if desired.

Wine suggestion: It is not necessary to use an expensive wine for a marinade of this style; a cask or flagon wine or an unfinished bottled wine would be the economical solution.

CRANBERRY CHUTNEY

2 oranges
water
½ cup red currant jelly
½ cup port wine
¾-1 cup sugar
1 teaspoon cinnamon
¼ teaspoon allspice
1 x 440 g (14 oz) jar whole cranberries
2 tablespoons red wine vinegar

Peel the rind in thin strips off the oranges, place in small quantity of water and heat until boiling; simmer 2-3 minutes, strain and cut into very thin shreds. Combine juice from the oranges, red currant jelly, wine, sugar, cinnamon and allspice in a saucepan; heat until boiling, then simmer 7-10 minutes. Add orange shreds and cranberries in syrup; stir until boiling, then simmer a further 5 minutes. Stir the vinegar through and set aside to cool.

Spoon into clean jars, seal and store in a cool place.

Note: Amount of sugar will depend upon sweetness of the syrup with the cranberries. If fresh cranberries are used increase sugar to 1½ cups.

Wine suggestions: A Ruby Port would give both flavour and colour to this special poultry accompaniment.

Desserts

JULIE'S MALLOW CREAM

1 packet instant pudding mix
1 cup milk
1 cup cream, whipped
1 cup marshmallows, halved
flavour variations (see below)

Empty contents of packet into a large bowl, whisk in the milk and set aside for a few moments to partially set. Stir cream and marshmallows through and fold in the flavour variety desired. Chill until ready to serve. Spoon into individual dessert bowls and decorate as desired. Serve.

Flavour variations:
Toffee Crunch: Use vanilla instant pudding and fold in crushed almond toffee with Maraschino, Kirsch or Cherry Heering liqueur.

Choco-Mint: Use lime instant pudding and fold in chopped chocolate pieces with Chocolate Peppermint, Creme de Cacao or Creme de Menthe liqueur.

Brazilian Whip: Use chocolate instant pudding and fold in crushed chocolate biscuits with Kahlua, Brazilian Coffee or Tia Maria liqueur.

Pine-orange Cream: Use orange instant pudding and fold in drained crushed pineapple and crushed coconut biscuits with Cointreau, Curaçao or Grand Marnier liqueur.

Che-berry Chill: Use strawberry instant pudding and fold in chopped strawberries with crushed meringue and Maraschino, Cherry Heering or Cherry Brandy liqueur.

Wine suggestion: Depending on the flavour variations added to the mixture serve a champagne or sparkling wine – sweetness as desired.

PEACH MELBA SLICE

1 packet shortbread biscuits
½ cup coconut
1 large can sliced peaches
1 cup rosé wine
½ cup raspberry jam
1 teaspoon grated orange rind
2 tablespoons orange juice
1 tablespoon arrowroot
60 g (2 oz) butter
½ teaspoon cinnamon
ice cream or whipped cream

Crush the shortbread biscuits, mix with the coconut and spread over the base of a shallow casserole; reserve ½ cup crumb mixture and set aside.

Drain peach slices and arrange in rows over the surface of the crumb mixture. Pour peach syrup into a saucepan, add wine, raspberry jam and orange rind and heat slowly until bubbling. Blend orange juice with arrowroot, add to boiling liquid and stir until thickened; spoon carefully over the peaches. Melt butter, add reserved crumb mixture and cinnamon and sprinkle over the top of the peaches and sauce. Bake in a moderate oven for 12-15 minutes; cut into slices and serve warm with ice cream or whipped cream.

Wine suggestion: A glass of sparkling wine — not too sweet so that it will match the hint of tartness from the raspberries — would be a fitting companion for this easy dessert.

HONEY ALMOND ICE

3 cups cream
6 egg yolks
1 cup honey
½ cup brown sugar
1 cup finely sliced almonds
3 tablespoons honey flavoured liqueur
4 egg whites
extra cream and almonds

Scald the cream, pour over beaten egg yolks, beating briskly; return to the saucepan, add honey and brown sugar and beat very slowly, stirring constantly until the mixture is of custard thickness. Do not allow to boil: for best control use a double saucepan. Allow to cool, stirring occasionally, then pour into freezer trays and partially freeze.

Transfer to a large bowl, beat briskly until smooth, fold in the stiffly beaten egg whites, almonds and the honey liqueur. Return to freezer trays, cover with plastic film and freeze quickly. Transfer trays to refrigerator about 30 minutes before serving to enable the ice cream to soften. Spoon into dessert glasses or bowls and decorate with extra cream and toasted almonds.

Wine suggestion: For an added touch, drizzle a spoonful of honey liqueur such as Drambuie over the dessert and serve with it one of the fruity spatlese or auslese white wines.

MARSALA CHOCOLATE MOUSSE

375 g (6 oz) dark semi-sweet chocolate
3 tablespoons coffee flavoured marsala wine
6 eggs, separated
1 cup raisins, softened in marsala
1 cup marshmallows, halved
whipped sweetened cream
chopped hazelnuts

Roughly chop the chocolate and place in top half of a double saucepan with the marsala wine; melt over hot (not boiling) water, stirring occasionally to blend. Stir egg yolks into the chocolate, remove from heat and cool slightly. Whip egg whites until stiff but not dry, gently fold the chocolate mixture through. Fold in the raisins and marshmallows, spoon into individual dessert dishes and chill well. Decorate with cream and hazelnuts just before serving.

Wine suggestion: This variation of the popular chocolate dessert would be enhanced by a glass of moselle with a full fruit flavour; or, for the really sweet tooth, a rich sauternes.

RHUBARB GINGER

6-8 stalks rhubarb
1-2 green apples
1 cup raisins
½ cup sultanas
1 teaspoon mixed spices
⅓ cup brown sugar
¼ cup orange juice
1 cup sparkling ginger wine
ice cream

Cut leaves from the rhubarb and chop stalks into short lengths; remove skin and core from the apples and slice thinly. Arrange the fruit in a well greased, ovenproof casserole, scatter the dried fruits over and sprinkle with combined spices and brown sugar. Combine the orange juice and ginger wine and pour over the fruits. Cover and cook in a slow oven for 30-35 minutes, until rhubarb is softened. Serve over scoops of ice cream.

Wine suggestion: A glass of the same sparkling ginger wine, or a glass of sweet sparkling wine, would be a festive accompaniment to this old-fashioned fruit dessert.

STRAWBERRIES SABAYON

2 punnets strawberries
1 egg
5 egg yolks
2 tablespoons sugar
2 teaspoons cornflour
½ cup white wine
pinch salt
¾ cup cream, chilled
cherry flavoured liqueur
red currant jelly

Reserve 5-6 of the best strawberries for decoration; remove stems from the remainder and cut into 4-5 slices, depending on size. Chill the whole strawberries. In top half of a glass double saucepan combine egg, egg yolks, sugar, cornflour and white wine, beat well to blend. Cook over simmering water, beating constantly, until mixture is thick and frothy. Remove from heat, beat vigorously for 1 minute, then transfer to a bowl standing in a larger bowl of crushed ice or ice cubes. Beat until the mixture is cold.

Whip salt and cream until thick, then fold into egg mixture together with drained sliced strawberries.

Roll a little cherry liqueur in the bowl of each dessert glass until the interior is coated. Spoon the strawberry mixture into each glass, piling high; chill. Warm the red currant jelly until almost liquid in consistency; do not over-heat. Dip the reserved strawberries in the jelly, swirling to coat all over; chill. Just before serving, decorate each dessert with a glazed strawberry. Serve with sponge finger biscuits or brandy crisps.

Wine suggestion: This spectacular dessert would be enhanced by a glass of champagne or sparkling wine – dry, semi-sweet or very sweet according to individual taste.

RAISIN CREAM CRÊPES

CRÊPES

½ cup plain flour
¼ teaspoon salt
1 teaspoon sugar
1 egg
1 egg yolk
1 tablespoon brandy
2 tablespoons melted butter, cooled
⅓-½ cup milk

FILLING

1 cup raisins
¼ cup brandy
1 strip lemon rind
250 g (8 oz) Ricotta cheese
60 g (2 oz) butter, softened
¼ cup icing sugar
2 egg yolks
½ cup chopped walnuts
pinch nutmeg or cinnamon
whipped cream, flavoured with brandy
extra nutmeg or cinnamon

Sift flour and salt into a basin, add sugar, beaten egg and egg yolk with brandy and gradually work the flour into the liquids. Lightly beat the butter through and set aside for 30 minutes. Add sufficient milk to beat to a thin cream. Cook thin pancakes as usual; set aside.

Cover raisins with warmed brandy, add lemon rind and set aside to plump; remove rind. Cream Ricotta with butter and icing sugar; add egg yolks and beat until smooth. Stir in raisins and walnuts and add nutmeg or cinnamon to taste.

Assemble the crêpes by spooning 2-3 tablespoons raisin filling onto centre of each; roll up and arrange in a heatproof dish; cover tightly. Just before serving, heat in a moderate oven for 5-6 minutes, only until filling commences to soften. Serve on dessert plates with a topping of flavoured cream; finish with a light sprinkling of nutmeg or cinnamon.

Wine suggestion: A good, sweet-tasting spätlese or auslese white wine, full of fruit flavour, will offset the richness of this dessert and leave a clean finish on the palate.

Chocolate Peppermint Torte, recipe on page 67.

BLUSHING PEACH DESSERT

½ cup port wine
½ cup red currant jelly
1 tablespoon sugar
¼ teaspoon powdered cinnamon
1 large can peach slices
10-12 glacé cherries
⅓ cup brandy
½ teaspoon Angostura bitters

Combine the port, red currant jelly, sugar, cinnamon and ½ cup of peach syrup in a chafing dish. Heat slowly, stirring constantly, until bubbling. Carefully add the drained peach slices and scatter the cherries over the top; heat through and simmer a few minutes. Combine brandy and bitters and pour carefully over the peaches. Allow to warm for 1 minute, ignite and allow to flame, shaking gently, until alcohol is evaporated and flames subside. Serve hot over scoops of ice cream or chilled whipped cream.

Wine suggestion: A liqueur brandy with higher alcohol content will provide more flames for a dramatic presentation. A Ruby Port would add more colour to the dish.

CHILLED FRUIT COMPOTE

1 honey dew or cantaloup melon
1 cup canned lychees in syrup
1 small can pear halves (approx. 5 halves)
1 small can red or black cherries
few strips orange rind
1 tablespoon finely chopped crystallized ginger
½ cup port wine
cream or ice cream

Remove skin and seeds from melon and scoop flesh into balls or cut into cubes. Drain syrup from canned fruits and place in a saucepan. Cut pear halves into quarters and combine all the fruits in a large bowl. Add orange rind strips and chopped ginger to the syrups; heat slowly until boiling, then continue to boil for 3-4 minutes to reduce by evaporation to about 1½ cups. Strain the syrup, stir in the port wine and set aside to cool.

Pour cooled syrup slowly over the combined fruits to coat all pieces, cover tightly and refrigerate until well chilled. Spoon into chilled dessert bowls with a slotted spoon and serve with whipped cream or ice cream.

Note: Vary the fruits as desired but avoid strong acid fruits which may conflict with the taste of the wine.

Wine suggestion: For still wine lovers, a sweet sauternes. For sparkling wine lovers, semi-sweet champagne.

MARMALADE MERINGUES

4 egg whites at room temperature
pinch salt
1 cup caster sugar
½ teaspoon cream of tartar
2 teaspoons orange flavoured liqueur
¾ cup orange marmalade
½ cup orange juice
extra 2 tablespoons orange flavoured liqueur
1 litre vanilla ice cream

Beat egg whites with the salt until very stiff. Gradually add almost all the sugar in tablespoon quantities, beating well between each addition. Combine remaining sugar with cream of tartar and beat into the egg whites. Slowly drizzle the liqueur into the egg whites, beating continuously. Spoon into a meringue bag with plain tube and pipe small snail shell shapes onto greased and corn-floured trays. Bake in a very slow oven for 1 hour; allow to cool and remove from trays.

Combine marmalade, orange juice and extra liqueur in a saucepan; heat slowly, stirring frequently until boiling.

To serve, sandwich two meringue shells together with a scoop of ice cream. Place onto a serving dish and spoon a little marmalade sauce over; serve immediately.

Wine suggestion: The contrasting flavours of sugar sweetness and citrus tang could be accompanied by a sweet fruity white wine, perhaps one made from Muscat Gordo Blanco grapes.

VACHERIN WITH KIRSCH

MERINGUE
5 egg whites
pinch salt
1 cup caster sugar

FILLING
4 egg yolks
2 tablespoons caster sugar
⅓ cup cherry flavoured liqueur
3 teaspoons gelatine
2 tablespoons hot water
2 cups cream, chilled
fruits

Beat egg whites with salt until very stiff; add half the sugar in three portions, beating in each portion thoroughly. Fold in remaining sugar. Place a 23 cm (9 in) round of aluminium foil on a biscuit tray, oil lightly and spread the meringue over. Scoop the centre of the meringue out slightly to resemble a pie case; place in a very slow oven and dry out for 1½ hours; set aside to cool slowly.

Combine egg yolks and sugar and beat until creamy; stir in liqueur and gelatine dissolved in water. When the mixture thickens slightly, fold in the stiffly whipped cream. Pile into meringue case and chill well.

To serve, top with fresh or canned fruit combinations as desired.

Wine suggestion: A glass of chilled spumante wine with its sweet fruit flavour would add a festive touch to this eye-catching dessert.

CITRUS SORBET

2 cups water
¾ cup crystal sugar
2 lemons
2 oranges
2 egg whites
extra 2 tablespoons sugar
2 tablespoons orange flavoured liqueur
mint sprigs

Pour water into a saucepan, carefully add sugar into the centre and slowly heat until sugar has dissolved. Bring to the boil and simmer steadily for 10 minutes to form a syrup. Add 2 thin strips of lemon rind and set aside until cold. Stir in combined fruit juices to measure 1 cup; strain through fine mesh and pour into freezer trays. Freeze until 'mushy'; turn into a chilled bowl.

Beat egg whites until stiff, add the extra sugar and beat well. Gradually drizzle in liqueur, beating continuously; fold into the citrus ice and return to freezer trays. Freeze until firm, stirring occasionally to prevent separation. About 30 minutes before serving, transfer to the refrigerator to soften gradually. Spoon into dessert glasses, decorate each with a mint sprig and serve immediately.

Wine suggestion: After a rich or heavy main meat course this refreshing ice dessert would go well with a glass of sparkling moselle or a sweet tasting pearl style wine.

CHOCOLATE MINT FONDUE

1 can sweetened condensed milk
1½ cups grated unsweetened chocolate
6-8 chocolate mint wafers
6-8 marshmallows
½ cup cream
2 tablespoons chocolate mint liqueur
chilled whipped cream

dippers: marshmallows, banana chunks,
    sponge finger pieces, butter cake,
    all well chilled

Combine condensed milk with chocolate, broken wafers and quartered marshmallows in a fondue pot. Heat, stirring constantly over hot water until all ingredients are melted and blended well. Add cream and liqueur and stir through. Transfer to table burner over low heat and allow to simmer very slowly for 5 minutes.

Guests spear desired 'dipper' ingredient onto a fondue fork, twist in the chocolate to coat, lift up and pause slightly to cool; then transfer to whipped cream bowl, twist again to coat before eating.

Wine suggestions: Use a chocolate mint liqueur such as Chocolate Peppermint or a mixture of Creme de Cacao and Creme de Menthe. Serve with a sweet sparkling wine, well chilled.

FRUIT CREAM FONDUE

fresh or canned fruits — pineapple, apricots,
    peaches, mandarin oranges, grapes,
    cherries
2 cups sour cream, chilled
2 tablespoons fruit brandy liqueur
1½ cups brown sugar

Prepare the fruits as required, providing chunks ready for eating; chill. Combine sour cream with brandy liqueur, place in a bowl over another bowl of crushed ice. Arrange the brown sugar in smaller bowls for individual servings.

Guests spear the fruit pieces onto fondue forks, dip in the sour cream and twist in the brown sugar to coat lightly.

Wine suggestions: Match the flavour of the brandy liqueur with the fruits selected for this recipe, apricot, peach, pineapple, strawberry, and so on. Serve a fruity sweet sparkling wine, well chilled.

FLAMING COFFEE SAUCE

1¼ cups hot strong black coffee
¼ cup brandy or Coffee Marsala
26-30 white marshmallows
1¼ cups cream
¼ cup coffee flavoured liqueur

Combine coffee and brandy in a saucepan; add half the marshmallows and stir over low heat until melted. Slowly add the cream, stirring constantly to blend through; heat until commencing to bubble.

Transfer to a heatproof serving jug with a wide mouth; reheat if necessary. Fold in the remaining marshmallows and quickly add the liqueur, pouring it over the back of a rounded spoon so that it stays on the top of the sauce. Ignite and use whilst flaming. To serve, spoon over scoops of vanilla ice cream or a mound of chilled whipped cream. Add raisins, glacé cherries or walnuts if desired.

Wine suggestions: A coffee flavoured liqueur such as Coffee Brazil, Kahlua, Continental Coffee, Cafe, Calypso Cream. Serve with a sweet fruity sauternes or a chilled pearl wine.

Pine-Berry Punch, recipe on page 76.

BRANDIED FRUITS

fruits – cherries, cumquats, strawberries,
   apricots, peaches or nectarines
caster sugar
brandy

Wash and dry fruit and prepare as desired; leave whole, cut in halves or slice. Prick cumquat skins with a needle point. Pack into clean jars sprinkling each layer with a little sugar. When jars are almost filled pour the brandy over the fruit to completely fill the jar. Seal tightly and store in a cool place at least one month. Use for desserts over ice cream.

Wine suggestions: A smooth brandy with no harsh qualities will complement the fruit and make a good syrup for later use.

BOTTLED BRANDY CURRANTS

4 cups sugar
2½ cups water
4-5 thin strips orange rind
5 cm (2 in) stick cinnamon
500 g (1 lb) good quality currants
¾ cup brandy
2 tablespoons orange flavoured liqueur

Place sugar and water in a large saucepan with orange rind and cinnamon stick; bring slowly to the boil and allow to boil for 2-3 minutes. Add currants, reduce heat and simmer for 8-10 minutes; remove from heat and allow to cool till warm. Remove the rind and cinnamon stick and add brandy and liqueur; spoon into clean jars and seal tightly. Store in a cool place for 2 weeks before use; use within 6 months. Serve chilled over ice cream or chilled whipped cream.
Note: A dried fruit medley of currants, sultanas, raisins, apricots, peaches and apples could be used in place of all currants if desired. Do not use fruit of distinctive flavour such as pineapple, figs, etc.

Wine suggestions: Orange flavoured liqueur such as Cointreau or Curaçao. Use a soft smooth brandy to form a subtle syrup.

PRUNES IN MUSCAT

500 g (1 lb) large dessert prunes
½ cup honey
⅓ cup water
5-6 thin strips orange rind
1½ cups muscat wine
2-3 tablespoons orange brandy liqueur

Carefully remove the stones from the prunes and re-shape; pack loosely into clean jars.
   Combine the honey, water and orange rind in a saucepan; bring slowly to the boil and simmer 2-3 minutes. Discard orange rind and allow to cool; add the muscat and liqueur and stir well. Pour the muscat syrup over the prunes in the jars to cover; seal tightly and shake gently to distribute the liquid. Set aside in a cool place for at least 3 months, turning upside down at intervals. Chill before serving.

Wine suggestions: A muscat with a rich fruit flavour, plus an orange brandy liqueur such as Grand Marnier, give a superb flavour to these prune tidbits.

Sweetmeats: Cakes and Biscuits

Wine or liqueur suggestions following each recipe in this section are those which can be used in the preparation and/or cooking of the foods. Wines for drinking with these foods will depend on the time and occasion they are being served.

MOCHA MARZIPAN BARS

1 pkt semi-sweet biscuits
1 cup walnut crumbs
½ cup chocolate pieces
½ cup condensed milk
2 teaspoons instant coffee
2 tablespoons chocolate liqueur

FILLING

2 cups icing sugar
½ cup almond meal
1 tablespoon lemon juice
1 large egg, beaten
almond essence

TOPPING

½ cup brown sugar
30 g (1 oz) butter
1 tablespoon liquid glucose
1 tablespoon chocolate liqueur
½ cup chocolate pieces
extra ½ cup walnut crumbs

Crush biscuits and combine with walnut crumbs; heat chocolate pieces over hot but not boiling water and carefully stir in the condensed milk, instant coffee and liqucur; mix until blended. Add to the biscuit-walnut mixture and press into the base of an aluminium foil lined and greased slab tin. Chill until firm.

Combine icing sugar with almond meal, moisten with lemon juice and beaten egg; add essence to taste and spread over the biscuit base, pressing down firmly. Place brown sugar, butter and glucose in the top of a double saucepan and heat over hot water until dissolved and well blended; add the chocolate liqueur and pieces and stir until dissolved. Quickly spread over the almond layer in the slab tin, scatter the extra walnut crumbs over and chill until set. Cut into small bars to serve.

Wine suggestions: Chocolate liqueur such as Creme de Cacao, Island Cream, Conticream.

CHOC-ORANGE CAKE

1 packet semi-sweet plain biscuits
125 g (4 oz) butter, melted
½ cup condensed milk
1 cup coconut
1 cup grated chocolate
1 tablespoon grated orange rind

ICING

30 g (1 oz) butter, melted
2 teaspoons condensed milk
2 tablespoons orange flavoured liqueur
2 tablespoons cocoa
1½ cups icing sugar
2 teaspoons grated orange rind
2 tablespoons coconut

Crush the biscuits into crumbs; combine butter and condensed milk. Mix together crumbs, coconut, grated chocolate and orange rind; add the buttermilk mixture and mix through. Press into a greased 20 cm (8 in) spring form pan and chill.

Combine melted butter for icing with condensed milk and liqueur. Sift cocoa and icing sugar into a bowl, add butter mixture and stir through. Heat over hot water for 2-3 minutes, spread onto the biscuit base evenly and allow to stand a few minutes. When commencing to set, sprinkle combined orange rind and coconut over the surface; chill again. Remove from the spring form pan and cut into small wedges for serving.

Wine suggestions: Use an orange flavoured liqueur such as Curaçao, Cointreau, Grand Marnier or Van der Hum.

BRANDY CREAM WAFERS

2 tablespoons golden syrup
60 g (2 oz) butter, softened
⅓ cup brown sugar
½ cup plain flour
1½ teaspoons ground ginger
½ teaspoon cinnamon
1½ cups cream, chilled
1 tablespoon icing sugar
2 tablespoons fruit brandy liqueur
extra icing sugar

Combine golden syrup, butter and brown sugar in a saucepan; stir over low heat until bubbling, remove from heat. Add sifted flour, ginger and cinnamon and stir well. Drop in teaspoons, well spaced, onto greased biscuit trays and bake in a moderate oven for 5-6 minutes. Remove from oven, carefully loosen on trays, cool and transfer to wire rack. Whip cream with icing sugar and brandy liqueur until very thick. Sandwich 2 wafer biscuits together with a generous amount of cream, dust icing sugar over and serve with fruit or cream desserts.

Wine suggestions: Fruit brandy liqueur could be Apricot, Peach or Cherry Brandy, Framboise or Kirsch.

CRUNCHY HAZELNUT BARS

1 cup finely chopped hazelnuts
1 cup finely crushed semi-sweet biscuits
1½ cups icing sugar
2 egg whites, lightly beaten
2 tablespoons coffee flavoured marsala wine
1¾ cups coarsely chopped chocolate
¾ cup condensed milk
60 g (2 oz) white shortening (Copha)

Combine hazelnuts, biscuit crumbs, icing sugar, egg whites and marsala; mix well and spread into a lined, well greased slab tin, pressing down firmly. Place chocolate in the top of a double saucepan, melt over hot but not boiling water. Add the condensed milk and chopped shortening; heat, stirring frequently, and cook for 3-4 minutes. Pour over the hazelnut layer, spreading evenly; cool and chill well. Cut into small bars for serving. Store, covered, in refrigerator.

Wine suggestions: Use coffee flavoured marsala or a mixture of Marsala and Coffee Brazil or Kahlua.

GOURMET FRUIT SLICE

1 cup glacé pineapple, cubed
1 cup glacé apricots, cubed
½ cup red glacé cherries
½ cup green glacé cherries
1 cup dates, stoned and halved
1 cup prunes, stoned and halved
½ cup glacé ginger pieces
2 cups Brazil nuts, halved
1 cup walnut pieces
2 tablespoons marmalade
3 tablespoons brandy
⅓ cup brown sugar
2 eggs
125 g (4 oz) butter, softened
⅔ cup plain flour
½ teaspoon baking powder
¼ teaspoon salt
2 tablespoons marmalade (extra)
1 tablespoon brandy (extra)

Combine fruits and nuts in a large bowl; pour the combined marmalade and brandy over and set aside 1-2 hours. Beat brown sugar and eggs until creamy, add butter and beat well; stir into fruit mixture. Sift the flour, baking powder and salt over the surface and fold through.

Line 2-3 bar or loaf tins with 2 thicknesses of aluminium foil, grease well and spoon equal portions fruit and nut mixture into each tin; press down firmly. Bake in slow oven 1¾-2¼ hours depending on size of tins; remove and brush the combined extra marmalade and brandy over the tops. Cool in the tins, remove and wrap well. Store in refrigerator.

Wine suggestion: Brandy gives a good mellow flavour and long keeping qualities to this glacé fruit confection.

Port Wine Fruit Cake, recipe on page 67. Gourmet Fruit Slice, recipe on page 64.

GLACÉ FRUIT SLICE

½ cup chopped glacé apricots
¼ cup chopped glacé pineapple
½ cup chopped red and green glacé cherries
⅓ cup sweet sherry
1 tablespoon spicy orange liqueur
375 g (12 oz) packaged cream cheese, softened
¼ cup icing sugar
½ cup coarsely grated chocolate
¼ cup chopped almonds
1½ cups crushed coconut biscuits
3 tablespoons melted butter, cooled
extra coconut biscuit crumbs

Combine chopped glacé fruits with sherry and liqueur, mixing well; cover and set aside overnight. Beat cream cheese with icing sugar until well blended; add the fruit and mix well. Combine grated chocolate with the almonds.

Mix the biscuit crumbs and butter together and sprinkle one-third into the base of a foil-lined greased loaf tin. Spread one-third of the fruit cream mixture over the top with half the chocolate and almonds. Continue adding the layers to use all the mixtures; press down firmly, cover with foil and chill well. Unmould, peel away foil and coat all surfaces with extra biscuit crumbs, pressing on firmly. Cut into slices for serving.

Wine suggestions: Use a spicy orange liqueur such as Strega, Chartreuse or Triple Sec.

CHOCOLATE ORANGE STRIPS

4-5 large oranges
water
1 cup sugar
½ cup water
2 tablespoons liquid glucose
1 cup chopped chocolate
30 g (1 oz) white shortening (Copha)
1 tablespoon orange flavoured liqueur

Cut the orange peel into lengthwise strips, slicing away as much of the white pith as possible; place in water, bring to the boil, then drain and dry.

Make a syrup of the sugar, ½ cup water and liquid glucose; boiling it to a soft ball stage, 110°C (230°F). Add the peel, simmer for 5 minutes, then drain off the syrup and spread out the peel to cool. Melt the chocolate, shortening and liqueur in the top of a double saucepan over hot but not boiling water. Carefully dip each orange peel strip in the chocolate, place on waxed paper to dry. Store in refrigerator.

Wine suggestions: Orange flavoured liqueur such as Curaçao, Cointreau or Grand Marnier.

ZABAGLIONE CHEESECAKE

1 packet semi sweet biscuits
125 g (4 oz) butter, melted
½ teaspoon each ground ginger and nutmeg
1 egg, beaten
5 egg yolks
½ cup sugar
¾ cup marsala
250 g (8 oz) cream cheese, at room temperature
2 cups ice cream
¾ cup cream, chilled and whipped
extra cream
extra nutmeg

Crush biscuits to fine crumbs and mix with butter, spices and beaten egg; press onto base and sides of a well greased 20 cm (8 in) spring form pan. Bake in a moderate oven for 10-12 minutes; remove, cool and chill.

Combine egg yolks and sugar in top half of a double saucepan, beat until thick, slowly pour in marsala, beating constantly. Cook the mixture, still beating constantly, over hot water until it thickens and increases in volume. Beat the cream cheese until soft and smooth, then gradually beat into the marsala mixture. Fold in the softened ice cream and cream; spoon into biscuit crust, cover and freeze.

Decorate with extra whipped cream. Sprinkle lightly with nutmeg and serve in slices.

Wine suggestions: The richness of a Marsala al'Uovo will complement the rich creamy filling.

CHOCOLATE PEPPERMINT TORTE

5 egg whites
½ cup caster sugar
2 tablespoons cornflour
1 tablespoon cocoa
125 g (4 oz) ground hazelnuts
2 tablespoons melted butter, cooled
¼ cup chocolate peppermint liqueur
1½ cups thickened cream, chilled
1 cup marshmallows, halved
1 cup coarsely grated chocolate
extra cream and chocolate
mint leaves
icing sugar

Cut out 3 x 20-23 cm (8-9 in) circles of aluminium foil and place on separate biscuit trays; grease each circle well. Whisk egg whites until stiff and dry; add caster sugar and beat until thick. Sift the combined cornflour, cocoa and ground hazelnuts over egg whites, pour melted butter over and lightly fold through to combine. Spread the mixture in equal amounts over the greased foil circles and bake in a moderate oven for 25-30 minutes. Allow to cool on the trays, then lift to a wire rack and peel away foil.

Sprinkle the chocolate peppermint liqueur over the surface of each meringue wafer, reserving a little for the filling; set aside. Whip cream until thick and firm; fold in the marshmallows and shaved chocolate and flavour with the reserved liqueur. Assemble the torte by sandwiching the wafers together with a generous filling of the chocolate cream between each layer. Decorate the top with extra cream, chocolate and mint leaves as desired, dusting a little icing sugar over the surface. Chill before serving.

Wine suggestions: Use chocolate peppermint liqueur or a mixture of Creme de Menthe and Creme de Cacao.

PORT WINE FRUIT CAKE

250 g (8 oz) butter
250 g (8 oz) brown sugar
1 cup milk
2 large eggs
¾ cup port wine
4 cups plain flour
1 teaspoon baking powder
1 teaspoon bicarbonate of soda
½ teaspoon each nutmeg and cloves
1 kg (2 lb) mixed dried fruits
½ cup dried apricots, finely chopped
½ cup seeded dates, finely chopped
½ cup walnuts or almonds, finely chopped
extra port wine

Beat butter and sugar in a large bowl until soft and creamy. Heat the milk until boiling; gradually whisk into the well beaten eggs, then return to the saucepan and stir over a very low heat until thickened; do not allow to boil. Whisk port wine into the egg custard, allow to cool slightly and add in gradual amounts to the butter cream; beat well after each addition. Fold in half the sifted dry ingredients and half the combined fruit and nuts; add the remaining quantities, stirring thoroughly but lightly.

Turn into a deep 23 cm (9 in) cake pan lined with double thickness aluminium foil, press down firmly and spread level. Bake in a very slow oven for 3½-4 hours. Remove from oven, brush surface with extra port wine and allow to cool in the pan. Wrap or cover tightly and store in a cool place at least one week before use.

Wine suggestions: Use a rich, fruity Tawny Port to team with the dried fruit flavours in this cake which is suitable for birthdays, weddings or Christmas.

Eating Outdoors

EGGS FOR SUNDAY BRUNCH

125 g (4 oz) butter
4-5 shallots or spring onions, chopped
1 thick ham steak, diced
½ cup ground almonds
¾ cup champagne or sparkling wine
6 large eggs, separated
¾ cup cream
1 teaspoon salt
¼ teaspoon pepper
2 teaspoons Worcestershire sauce
5-6 large puff pastry shells or
   5-6 buttered toast slices
2-3 tomatoes

Heat butter in a large frying pan, preferably over barbecue coals; add shallots and ham and sauté until ham pieces are slightly crisp. Add the ground almonds and cook, stirring constantly, a further 1-2 minutes. Pour champagne over and pull to the side of the coals to simmer for 2-3 minutes.

Beat egg yolks, cream, salt, pepper and sauce together; fold in the stiffly beaten egg whites and add to champagne mixture. Cook, stirring constantly, until eggs are almost set; spoon into heated pastry shells or over buttered toast and serve with a garnish of sliced tomatoes.

Wine suggestion: A special dish which would be ideal for a champagne breakfast. So why not champagne – or sparkling wine?

BARBECUED PACKET STEAK

2 kg (4 lb) piece yearling steak, flank, round,
   chuck or topside
½ cup vegetable oil
⅓ cup red wine
1 tablespoon red wine vinegar
1 tablespoon soy sauce
1 teaspoon onion salt
5-6 peppercorns, crushed
2 bay leaves
2 cloves garlic (optional)
250 g (8 oz) open flat mushrooms
1 can mushroom soup, approx. 1¼ cups
chopped parsley
seasonings as desired

Trim the thick piece of steak of any excess fat, beat lightly with a mallet but do not flatten. Combine the following 8 ingredients and whisk well to blend; pour over the steak in a glass or china dish and turn the steak a few times to thoroughly moisten. Cover tightly and refrigerate for several hours, turning the steak from time to time.

Prepare a double thickness square of heavy duty aluminium foil large enough to enclose the steak and seal tightly. Grease or oil the foil well, place the lightly drained steak in the centre and arrange whole mushrooms on top; fold the foil over the top and seal securely. Lift onto bars or hotplate of a heated barbecue and cook for 15-20 minutes, turning occasionally to cook evenly. Carefully lift to one side, open foil, lift out steak and place it directly on bars or hotplate to achieve the seared effect and flavour. Cook to desired degree, turning once or twice.

Turn the mushrooms and juices into a fireproof pan, add soup and stir to combine with ¼ cup of the marinade liquid; heat until bubbling. Lift steak onto a heated platter, sprinkle with parsley and carve in thin slices against the grain and with a slight slanting angle to the knife; season slightly. Serve at once with mushrooms and sauce spooned over.

Wine suggestion: This barbecue 'steak with a difference' would be complemented by a red wine of light to medium body and good fruity aroma – a good commercial wine of moderate price.

BEEF BREAD LOAF DE LUXE

1.5 kg (3 lb) beef fillet
pepper
60 g (2 oz) butter or substitute
¼ cup brandy
2-3 rashers bacon, rind removed
125 g (4 oz) mushrooms
250 g (8 oz) soft liverwurst
extra butter or substitute
2 tablespoons red wine
1 long round loaf Italian or milk bread
chopped parsley

Trim beef fillet and rub surface with freshly ground pepper; tie with string in few places to help retain shape. Heat butter in large pan, add fillet and sear meat on all sides over high heat; carefully pour brandy over, warm and ignite. Roll meat around in the pan to absorb flavours. When flames die down, continue cooking the meat over lowered heat for 10-15 minutes, turning frequently. Lift meat out and set aside.

Add finely chopped bacon to pan and fry until fat is transparent. Add finely chopped mushrooms and cook a further 2-3 minutes, then stir in liverwurst and blend through, adding 1 tablespoon melted butter and wine.

Cut a slice off the top of the bread loaf lengthwise, scoop out the soft centre to within 2.5 cm (1 inch) of the crust. Brush melted butter over the inside of the loaf including the top crust; sprinkle well with salt and pepper. Spread a layer of the liverwurst mixture over the inside surface of the loaf and lid. Remove string from the fillet and place it in the loaf; sprinkle with parsley. Cover with the top crust, place on greased aluminium foil and roll up, securing the top and ends.

Thirty minutes before serving place the loaf in a moderately hot oven or over moderately-heated coals of a barbecue and heat through, turning frequently. To serve, fold back the foil, lift onto a platter and slice through the loaf in 2.5 cm (1 in) pieces. Serve with vegetables or salad as desired.

Wine suggestion: A top quality claret style wine in flagon or cask would team successfully with this gourmet meat loaf – one with a pleasant bouquet and soft mellow palate.

PORK SAUSAGE STICKS

1.5 kg (3 lb) pork sausages
water
1 tablespoon curry powder
1 teaspoon salt
½ cup honey
½ cup sweet sherry
60 g (2 oz) butter or substitute
2 cups crushed potato crisps

Blanch sausages in water, allow to cool. Combine the next 5 ingredients in a saucepan, heat until the honey softens and the butter melts to blend. Pierce each sausage lengthwise with a butcher's wooden skewer to act as a handle whilst grilling; cover the skewer end with aluminium foil for easy handling. Brush the honey-sherry mixture onto each sausage, coating it well; grill over barbecue coals on moderate heat, turning frequently, for 10-15 minutes. Turn each sausage in potato crisps to cover and serve hot on the skewer.

Wine suggestion: Basically a barbecue treat for juniors but as an adult snack these crunchy sausages could be served with a chilled white or rosé wine.

SIZZLING PORK SPARERIBS

15-18 thick pork spareribs
3 tablespoons brown sugar
2 teaspoons mustard
½ cup sweet vermouth
3-4 cloves garlic, crushed
olive oil
salt and pepper
1 cup white wine
1 tablespoon chopped fresh thyme

Rub the pork spareribs all over with a mixture of brown sugar, mustard, vermouth and garlic; stand aside 1 hour. Arrange the meat on long skewers, using 2 paralled skewers in each series of spareribs for ease of turning, etc. Brush generously with olive oil and sear over heated barbecue coals for a few minutes on each side; season well.

Combine the white wine with any remaining vermouth mixture and the chopped thyme (use more vermouth mixture if necessary). Continue cooking over lowered heat, brushing frequently with the white wine mixture and turning as required, for a further 20-25 minutes, until cooked through. Remove from the skewers onto well heated platters and serve immediately with crusty bread or vegetables.

Note: If preferred, bake in a very hot oven for 10 minutes, lower heat to moderate for remainder of cooking time.

Wine suggestion: A full flavoured white burgundy style wine with a touch of residual sugar but clean soft finish (in bottle or bulk) would go well with these slightly sweet coated pork ribs.

ROAST-ROTISSERIE PORK

2.5 kg (5 lb) loin of pork
500 g (1 lb) sausage meat
2 tablespoons dry mustard
¾ cup dry sherry
½ cup soy sauce
2 cloves garlic, crushed
2 teaspoons ground ginger
vegetable oil

Ask butcher to bone, roll and tie the loin of pork securely, placing sausage meat down the centre. Rub mustard well into skin of pork and place in a shallow dish. Combine dry sherry with soy sauce, garlic and ground ginger and pour over pork, turning well to coat all sides. Set aside for 1-2 hours, turning pork occasionally and spooning marinade up over the surface.

Lift pork roll onto a large piece of aluminium foil, pour marinade liquid over and fold the foil loosely over the top. Place in a baking dish and roast in moderately slow oven for 2 hours, turning the pork roll occasionally to cook more evenly; remove from oven and set aside to cool. Place in refrigerator until required.

When ready to barbecue, spear the pork roll onto spit or fork of rotisserie, secure ends with clamps. Brush all over with vegetable oil and balance on the barbecue; roast over low heat coals for 1-1¼ hours or until well cooked, brushing with oil at frequent intervals. Remove from rotisserie, rest for 10 minutes before cutting into thick slices for serving.

Wine suggestion: This mouth-watering roast pork roll would be wonderful accompanied by a good red wine made from Cabernet Sauvignon grapes, with fruit character and a pleasant touch of oak.

BARBECUED CHICKEN MARYLAND

5-6 small chicken maryland pieces (thigh and
   leg)
1 onion, finely chopped
1 tablespoon prepared mustard
2 teaspoons chopped fresh thyme
1 tablespoon tomato chutney or paste
2 teaspoons Worcestershire sauce
1 teaspoon salt
¼ teaspoon pepper
¾ cup vegetable oil
¾ cup dry sherry or vermouth

SAUCE
60 g (2 oz) butter or substitute
½ cup chopped almonds
½ cup ground almond meal
reserved marinade
extra dry sherry or vermouth
lemon juice

Trim chicken pieces as required and prick the surface with a pointed knife in several places; place in a glass or china bowl. Mix onion with the next 6 ingredients, pressing firmly to combine all flavours. Add oil and sherry and blend thoroughly; pour over the chicken pieces and mix through. Cover and set aside 1-2 hours, turning occasionally. Drain chicken pieces, reserving the marinade. Place chicken pieces on grill or hotplate over barbecue coals on low heat and cook, turning frequently, for 25-30 minutes. Lift off the coals when tender and serve with the following sauce.

Sauce: Heat butter in a small saucepan and sauté chopped almonds until browned but not burnt. Stir in almond meal with the reserved marinade and heat until bubbling; add extra wine and lemon juice to taste.

Wine suggestion: These chicken pieces would have added appeal when accompanied by a white wine made from the Sauvignon Blanc grape, full and fruity with a firm acid finish.

SKEWERED BEEF AND ONIONS

1 kg (2 lb) rump or yearling topside, in one
   piece
3 tablespoons soy sauce
½ cup red wine
1 tablespoon honey, slightly warmed
2 cloves garlic, crushed
¼ teaspoon chilli powder
¼ teaspoon pepper
2 tablespoons vegetable oil
18-20 tiny white onions, skinned
salted water
extra red wine

Cut meat into equal sized chunky pieces and place in a glass or china bowl. Combine soy sauce and red wine with honey, garlic, chilli powder, pepper and vegetable oil and mix well. Pour over the steak pieces and mix through; cover and marinate for 1-2 hours, turning meat from time to time. Meanwhile parboil onions in salted water for 7-10 minutes, remove and allow to cool.

At cooking time thread meat chunks and onions onto long skewers, leaving a little space in between to enable the foods to cook more evenly. Add extra red wine to remaining marinade to bring to at least ½ cup. Place skewers over barbecue coals and grill, turning frequently and basting with the marinade, for 15 minutes or until cooked to desired degree. Serve hot.

Wine suggestion: A flagon or cask red wine, one that is rich and full of flavour, would be suitable both for the cooking and to serve with this beef dish.

Terrace Chicken and Rice, recipe on page 75.

HOT CAMEMBERT ROLLS

1 cup white wine
1 small Camembert cheese
1 cup shredded mild processed cheese
1 tablespoon chopped parsley, chives, basil,
    oregano or marjoram as desired
125 g (4 oz) butter
10-12 small white bread rolls

Heat wine in a small saucepan until hot but not boiling; lower heat. Remove rind from the Camembert and cut into chunky pieces; add to the wine with the processed cheese in portions, stirring until melted and blended through; do not overheat. Add parsley or other herbs with pieces of butter and mix well. Cut a slash into each bread roll and spread in a generous amount of the cheese-wine mixture. Close slash, wrap each roll in aluminium foil squares and reheat around edges of barbecue fire or in a moderate oven when required.

Note: Add extra savoury seasonings if desired, according to taste and accompanying foods.

Wine suggestion: Use a light white wine in the cheese mixture so that it will not dominate the flavour of the cheeses. Serve a wine according to tastes of other foods.

SPANISH RICE MEDLEY

2-3 chicken breasts
500 g (1 lb) fresh prawns
2 white onions, sliced
1 red and 1 green capsicum, seeded and sliced
125 g (4 oz) salt pork or bacon
2-3 continental style hot sausages
water
4 tablespoons olive oil
salt, pepper and paprika
2 cups long grain rice
1 cup white wine
1 cup frozen green peas, thawed
¼ teaspoon saffron (optional)
2 tablespoons chopped parsley or shallots

Remove bones and skin from chicken breasts, cut meat into strips; remove shells from prawns and devein if required. Slice onions and capsicums thinly; cut salt pork into strips. Blanch sausages in water, drain and cut in 2.5 cm (1 in) diagonal slices, reserve water. Heat oil in a large frying pan, add chicken strips, prawns, onions and capsicums, salt pork and sausages in succession; fry each to brown lightly and remove to set aside.

Add salt, pepper, paprika and rice to the pan, stirring to coat rice grains but not allowing to brown. Return chicken, onion, capsicum, salt pork and sausages to the pan, stirring well. Pour white wine and 3½ cups hot water (from sausages) over; cover and simmer for 15 minutes; add prawns and peas. Soak saffron in little hot water, strain and add to the pan, stirring carefully. Cook a further 2-3 minutes; serve hot with parsley garnish.

Wine suggestion: A Paella style buffet dish ideal for casual eating. Serve a well developed white burgundy that has full rounded flavour with a pleasant soft finish.

TERRACE CHICKEN AND RICE

1 x 2 kg (4 lb) boiling chicken
1 x 220 g (7oz) can tuna in brine
1 x 40g (1½ oz) can anchovies
2 cups water
2 cups white wine
2-3 gherkins or 1 dill pickle, sliced
1 carrot, sliced
2 stalks celery, sliced
2 white onions, chopped
2-3 sprigs parsley
1 teaspoon peppercorns
2 cups long grain rice
water
3-4 shallots or spring onions
salt and pepper
egg mayonnaise
lemon juice
capers

Place cleaned, trimmed chicken in a large saucepan with the following 10 ingredients and bring slowly to the boil; remove any scum from surface, cover and simmer for 1 hour. Test chicken for tenderness, continue cooking as required; set aside to cool. Lift out chicken, return liquid to heat and simmer for a further 30-40 minutes. Strain liquid through fine mesh, measure off 1 cup liquid and return remainder to a low heat to reduce to a pulp consistency.

Cook rice in the 1 cup liquid plus water as required until just softened. Add shallots and sprinkling of salt and pepper as required; allow to cool. Cut chicken into serving sized pieces, removing skin and bones. Combine 1½ cups mayonnaise with each cup of the stock 'pulp'; season with lemon juice.

To serve, arrange rice on a large platter, place pieces of chicken in the centre and spoon mayonnaise mixture over the pieces; garnish with capers. Arrange salad garnishes around edge of platter and serve cold.

Wine suggestion: Choose a good quality cask or flagon riesling, one that is fresh and clean, full flavoured, but well balanced, to complement this interesting chicken dish.

PINEAPPLE TROPICALE

2 large ripe pineapples
1 large pawpaw
1 large punnet strawberries
2 oranges
icing sugar
cherry flavoured liqueur

Halve the pineapples lengthwise through tops and carefully cut out the flesh with a small grapefruit knife; trim the skin and leaves neatly, cover and chill. Remove core from the pineapple flesh, cut flesh into chunks. Cut skinned seeded pawpaw into similar sized pieces. Wash and remove hulls from strawberries, cut in halves. Combine all the fruit in a large bowl.

Squeeze juice from oranges and add icing sugar to taste, depending on tartness of oranges and other fruits. Mix with equal quantity of liqueur and pour over the fruits; set aside for 1 hour, turning carefully from time to time to distribute the juices. The fruits can be chilled but should be removed from the refrigerator at last an hour before serving to allow flavours to develop fully.

For serving, pile the fruits into the pineapple halves and arrange on large platters, decorated perhaps with tropical leaves and flowers.

Wine suggestion: Make sure the pineapples are ripe and sweet to do full justice to a Rhine Riesling wine from grapes grown in colder, higher regions with a little acid but full flavour.

Drinks

CHILL CHASER

3 cups water
1 tablespoon sugar
½ teaspoon ground cinnamon
5-6 cloves
1 tablespoon lemon or orange juice
1 bottle red wine
2 tablespoons brandy *or*
1 tablespoon spicy flavoured liqueur

Combine water, sugar, cinnamon, cloves and lemon juice in a large enamel lined saucepan; bring slowly to the boil and simmer 5 minutes. Add the red wine and when almost bubbling again, pour in the brandy or liqueur. Pour into a heated jug and serve in heated glass mugs.

Wine suggestion: Use a fruity, full bodied red wine from a flagon or cask to allow for extra serves and a spicy flavoured liqueur such as Benedictine or Galliano.

PINE-BERRY PUNCH

3 x 440 g (15 oz) cans crushed pineapple
6 cloves
1 piece stick cinnamon
2 pieces crystallized or glacé ginger
1 cup water
1½ cups orange juice
½ cup lemon juice
1.5 litres (2 bottles) sauternes wine
2 bottles lemonade
12-15 strawberries, cut in quarters

Place the cans of crushed pineapple in freezer for 2-3 hours. Put the cloves, cinnamon and ginger with water in a saucepan, bring to the boil, stirring occasionally, to extract the flavours from the spices; allow to cool and strain through fine mesh. Open pineapple cans and place blocks of crushed pineapple in a punch bowl, add spiced water, orange and lemon juices and wine. Just before serving add the lemonade and quartered strawberries and stir well. Serve in tall glasses.

Wine suggestion: A flagon sauternes would be ideal for this light refreshing punch, with sufficient leftovers to make a second bowl.

SODA SLING

For each glass:
2 crushed ice cubes
1 measure sweet vermouth
1 dash Angostura bitters
1 squeeze lemon
soda, icy cold

Place crushed ice cubes in a tall glass; add vermouth, bitters and lemon and stir to mix well. Fill the glass with soda and serve.

Wine suggestion: Bitters and lemon add to the spicy sweet vermouth for this longer thirst-quencher drink.

PINK PINK LADY

1 x 440 g (14 oz) can sliced beetroot
1½ cups white wine
1 tablespoon white wine vinegar
¼-½ teaspoon Tabasco sauce
1 tablespoon grated horseradish
1 x 300 ml carton sour cream

Combine all ingredients in an electric blender in 3-4 quantities and blend for a few seconds; chill well. Serve in small glasses at the commencement of a meal.

Wine suggestion: Choose a young fresh wine with acid content to give a biting taste to this aperitif cocktail drink.

CHOC-COFFEE LIQUEUR

2 cups water
4 cups sugar
60 g (2 oz) instant coffee
60 g (2 oz) unsweetened chocolate
1 vanilla bean
1 x 700 ml bottle brandy
2-3 tablespoons orange brandy liqueur

Pour water into a saucepan, add sugar and heat slowly until sugar dissolves. Add instant coffee, chopped chocolate and vanilla bean and continue to heat, stirring to blend the mixture, for 1 minute. Remove from heat, allow to cool and add the brandy and liqueur; mix thoroughly. Pour into clean bottles, seal tightly and stand in a cool place for at least 2 months before use.

Wine suggestions: Use a liqueur brandy, and an orange brandy liqueur such as Grand Marnier.

GINGER TINGLE

2 cups strong hot tea
1 cup crystal sugar
2 cups grapefruit juice
1 cup orange juice
2 cups ice cubes
2 bottles ginger sparkling wine
mint sprigs
orange slices

Combine the hot tea and sugar and reboil until the sugar has dissolved; strain if necessary and cool. Add the fruit juices to the tea in a large container and chill thoroughly. Just before serving, pour the fruit-tea mixture over ice cubes in a large punch bowl; add 1 bottle of sparkling wine and reserve the second to 'top up' the drink as it loses its effervescence. Decorate the side of each tall glass with mint sprigs and orange slices and three-parts fill each glass for serving.

Note: Dry ginger ale and lemonade may replace the sparkling wine for serving to children.

Wine suggestion: Use a ginger sparkling wine such as Yum Sing or substitute a sparkling wine and add chopped crystallized ginger to taste.

ICED TOMATO CUP

3 cups tomato juice, chilled
1 cup natural yoghurt, chilled
½ cup chopped celery
½ cup chopped onion
2 tablespoons dry vermouth
2 teaspoons Angostura bitters
salt and pepper
crushed ice
chopped chives or parsley

Combine the first six ingredients in an electric blender in 3 or 4 quantities and blend a few seconds. Add salt and pepper to taste and pour over crushed ice in tall glasses; garnish and serve.

Wine suggestion: Dry vermouth plus an aromatic bitters provide plenty of spicy flavour for this aperitif drink before a summer meal.

Appendix– About Wine

In order to know which wines will taste best with certain foods it is necessary to understand a few things about the various types of wine.

For those embarking on the exciting discovery of the enjoyment of wine in food and wine with food the following information will be useful.

Generally speaking wines fit into five classes or categories: aperitif or appetiser wines; white table wines; red table wines; sweet desert wines and sparkling wines.

Aperitif or Appetiser Wines

These are so called because of their use at cocktail time or before a meal. They consist mainly of sherry and vermouth in tastes varying from sweet to dry. They can be served straight from the bottle, chilled or with ice cubes in 60 ml (2 oz) portions, or combined with soda or carbonated drinks to make mixtures of varying proportions.

White Table Wines

These vary in colour from light to deeper gold and in taste from sweet to dry or delicate to full in flavour. They should be served chilled but not icy cold in 150 ml (5 oz) portions. Excessive chilling tends to nullify the delicate flavours in the wine. They are usually served during a meal, teaming best with light or mild flavoured foods.

Red Table Wines

Colour variations from light red to purple, brick to brownish red and taste changes from light to full bodied, soft to astringent are all indicative of the range of differences accorded to red wine styles, grape varieties and growing areas. They should be served at a temperature of 18°C (65°F) — the best conditions — and even slightly chilled in summer. Serve in 125 ml (4 oz) portions during the meal, ideally with fuller flavoured foods.

Sweet Dessert Wines

These include the sweeter fortified wines such as port, muscat, marsala and madeira and should be served with desserts or after a meal with sweetmeats or cheese. Serve at cool cellar temperatures of approximately 18°C (65°F) in 60 ml (2 oz) portions.

Sparkling Wines

Embracing the bottle-fermented champagnes, tank-fermented sparkling wines and effervescent carbonated wines, these popular varieties range from very dry to excessively sweet in flavour and can be served before, during or after meals. Serve well chilled in 150 ml (5 oz) portions.

FORTIFIED WINES

Marsala: a sweet, thick syrupy wine with varying flavour elements such as vanilla, egg and coffee.

Muscat: a sweet dessert wine of two varieties. White: pronounced flavour of raisins. Brown: wood matured for richness of taste and colour.

Madeira: a sweet dessert wine of two varieties. Sercial: sweet with slight bitter flavour; dry finish. Malmsey: rich full flavour and aroma; sweet taste and finish.

Sherries:

Cream: a fruity sweet-tasting wine, rich and full-bodied with a mellow, clinging after-taste.

Oloroso: a semi-sweet dessert style wine of rich, deep colour and slight oak flavour; smooth finish.

Amontillado: a medium-dry, subtle-tasting aperitif wine, good fruit flavour and slightly dry, cleansing finish.

Flor: a dry aperitif wine with a distinctive delicate aroma and ''nutty'' flavour; crisp finish. The term ''fino'' for some flor sherries indicates ''pale''.

Port Wines:

White: a sweet wine with slight dry finish.

Ruby: a light but full, fruity wine with slightly astringent finish.

Tawny: a rich sweet wine taking colour from wood ageing; full fruit flavour with no lingering sweetness.

Vintage: A sweet premium wine usually allowed to age in the bottle to give deep colour, fruity taste and firm astrindent finish.

Vermouths:

Bianco: a white to light golden wine, light and fruity with aromatic nose and flavour; crisp finish.

Dry: a white apertif wine flavoured with herbs and spices; delicate yet sophisticated taste and finish.

Sweet: a deep red wine with a full-bodied blend of herbs and spices for extra flavour.

WINE STYLES

Sauternes: a sweet white wine of two categories. Young: a light clean wine with a rich fruity flavour and crisp dry finish. Old: a deeper golden coloured wine, sweet in the mouth but with no excessive after-taste.

Moselle: a delicate white wine with pronounced fruity flavour often mistaken for sugar; slight degree of sweetness on the tongue but with a low acid finish.

White Burgundy: a full flavoured white wine with strong fruit taste and bouquet; mellow with a smooth, lingering finish.

Hock: a light dry white wine with a delicate but fragrant bouquet; fresh but flowery palate taste with a crisp, clean finish.

Chablis: a light, fresh white wine with generous but delicate bouquet and taste; distinctive flint finish.

Riesling: a crisp, dry white with a generous full fruit aroma and flavour; slight acid provides clean, fresh finish.

Rosé: a pink to light red wine varying in sweetness, fresh fruit flavour; sometimes slightly spritzig, slight tanin finish.

Burgundy: a rich, soft tasting red wine with good fruit flavour and nose; shows oak character but lacking astringency.

Claret: a light red wine, varying in colour and aroma; soft taste but tanin content provides firm astringent finish.

SPARKLING WINES
"Champagnes"

Brut: a classic white wine with delicate bouquet and taste; clean, very dry finish.

Dry: a white wine with slight fruit flavour, refreshing clean finish.

Demi-Sec: a white wine with a slight degree of sweetness; good fruit flavour; clean, slightly sweet finish.

Sec: a white wine with a full fruity bouquet and taste; exceptionally sweet finish.

Other Sparkling Wines

Pearl Wine: an effervescent wine, slight aroma and sweet taste, sweet to very sweet finish.

Spumante: a white wine with the unmistakable bouquet and flavour of fresh grapes; hint of sweetness with refreshing finish.

Moselle: white wine with a delicate fruit bouquet and flavour; slightly sweet finish.

Burgundy: a sparkling red wine, good fruit flavour and aroma with dry finish and after-taste.

Index